ON THE ORIGIN OF LANGUAGE

D1363834

ON THE
ORIGIN OF LANGUAGE

Jean-Jacques Rousseau
ESSAY
ON THE ORIGIN OF LANGUAGES

Johann Gottfried Herder
ESSAY
ON THE ORIGIN OF LANGUAGE

Translated, with afterwords, by
JOHN H. MORAN *and* ALEXANDER GODE
Introduction by Alexander Gode

THE UNIVERSITY OF CHICAGO PRESS
CHICAGO AND LONDON

The University of Chicago Press, Chicago 60637
The University of Chicago Press, Ltd., London

09 08 07 06 05 04   8 9 10 11

*Originally published 1966 by Frederick Ungar Publishing
Co., Inc.*

Library of Congress Cataloging-in-Publication Data

Main entry under title:

On the origin of language.

   Reprint, Originally published: New York : F. Ungar,
1966.
   Bibliography: p.
   Contents: Essay on the origin of languages /
Jean-Jacques Rousseau—Essay on the origin of
language / Johann Gottfried Herder.
   1. Language and languages—Origin—Addresses,
essays, lectures. I. Moran, John H. II. Code,
Alexander, 1906–1970. III. Rousseau, Jean-Jacques,
1712–1778. Essai sur l'origine des langues. English.
1986. IV. Herder, Johann Gottfried, 1744–1803.
Abhandlung über den Ursprung der Sprache. English.
1986.
P116.05   1986   401   85–20945
ISBN 0–226–73012–3 (paper)

INTRODUCTION

Jean-Jacques Rousseau (1712-1778) is frequently labeled
"The Father of Romanticism." So is Johann Gottfried
Herder (1744-1803). This need not lead to a contest in
paternity, but it could be used as the basis of a penetrating comparative study of the significance of romanticism in France and Germany respectively. In any event,
what the two romanticisms—and the two Fathers of
Romanticism—have in common are the spirit of revolt
against derivative convention and the spirit of dedication
to things primordial, to ancestries and origins, to Nature.

Indeed, it is by no means a coincidence that both Rousseau and Herder gave much thought to language, including its whence and wherefore, for both recognized
language as a *sine qua non*, as the natural lifeblood of
human culture and social demeanor in all its forms. Both
alluded repeatedly to the problem of the origin of language in works other and earlier than the essays wholly
devoted to the subject.

It is virtually certain that Rousseau knew nothing of
Herder. On the other hand, Herder was well acquainted
with Rousseau's writings, though it should be noted that
where, in his own essay on the origin of language, Herder
argued against Rousseau's views, he did not refer to the
latter's parallel essay but to the allusions to the subject
found in Rousseau's *Discourse on the Origin and Bases
of the Inequality among Men* of 1754.

The joint presentation, in the present volume, of Rousseau's and Herder's essays on linguistic origins appeared meaningful not only by reason of the striking equivalency of the positions assigned to the two men by history at major turning points in the continuity of thought in their respective countries. It also suggested itself by virtue of the fact that these essays represent the two major possible approaches to the problem, as is neatly reflected in their titles. Herder's essay is concerned with "The Origin of Language," that is, with the genesis of the faculty of speech, while Rousseau's (among other things) treats of "The Origin of Languages" in their diversity. This distinction runs through the history of the literature on linguistic origins, corresponding to the questions of how man acquired the faculty of speech and of how—the faculty being given or assumed—he came to make use of it.

There are no known facts to support a direct answer to either of these questions, and both approaches lead far afield into the realms of free-wheeling philosophical speculation. In answer to the question of how man acquired his characteristic faculty of speech, there is at least the possibility—though not the necessity—of calling, with unassailable succinctness, on God's creative omnipotence. Much of Herder's essay, by the way, is concerned with the rejection of this facile explanation. He found it quite as unphilosophical and even as theologically unsound as later generations found it unscientific.

With the coming of age of the science of linguistics in the nineteenth century, the question of the origin of language as such fell into disrepute. The Linguistic Society of Paris, which was founded in 1866, had in its bylaws the provision that it would not, under any circumstances, accept any kind of communication on the subject of the origin of language. And most scholars in the field of linguistics contented themselves with a resigned *ignoramus, ignorabimus.*

There were exceptions, especially during the early decades when it was still possible for a scholar in linguistics to be simultaneously a philosopher and a historian. A little later there was Max Müller, here mentioned by name because it was he who set up the famous classification of theories concerning the origin of language distinguishing the "bow-wow," the "pooh-pooh," and the "yo-he-ho" groups. In the "bow-wow" theories, human language is assumed to have begun as the imitation of animal sounds. According to the "pooh-pooh" theories, the earliest human words were emotional outcries. Lastly, the "yo-he-ho" theories stipulate that man began to speak in response to the requirements of concerted action.

A striking feature of Müller's scheme of classification is that it has no room for theories other than those providing mechanical patterns for the development of language by a creature already endowed with the requisite faculties. It cannot accommodate theories according to which the gift of tongues was a gift of God, nor any in which the bestowing of that gift and not just its subsequent exploitation was taken to be what was in need of an explanation.

In the twentieth century the question of the origin of language has continued to occupy the minds of enthusiastic amateurs who often seem only too eager to rush into print with what they consider to be a novel theory.

A special case is that of the great Danish linguist, Jespersen, who proposed to tackle the problem by tracing through meticulous research the documented development of all accessible languages since historical times and—guided by the assumption that the observed trends prevailed at all times—beyond the beginnings of history into the darkness beshrouding the ultimate origins. This approach differs in its degree of sophistication magnificently from that of the bow-wowists and their pooh-poohing and yo-he-hoing colleagues, but it cannot, almost by definition of purpose, probe any more satisfactorily the origin either of man's need or of his desire for verbal communication with his fellows. Indeed it does not pretend to be able to do so.

A new dimension would be added to both the question of the origin of language itself and to the methodological possibilities of solving it, if more were known about the language or languages of animals. So far most critical observers have come to suspect that the phenomena covered by the convenient term of "animal language" differ in kind, not just in degree of evolutionary maturity, from human language.

Perhaps the first and foremost difficulty is that we do not in fact know what human language is. One excuse for the ignorance to which the best among us plead guilty is that there are no primitive languages, that is, languages which represent a less advanced phase in evolution by descent and the comparative study of which might provide us with a sense of direction. This adds indeed mightily to the recalcitrance of the problem of the origin of language and languages.

It is a sobering thought that we cannot look back on Rousseau and Herder as naïve pioneers in matters which we meanwhile have learned to handle with consummate mastery and wisdom. They may not have solved the problem they set out to solve, but there remains much we can learn from them.

BIBLIOGRAPHIC NOTE

Various French and German works published before the composition of Rousseau's and Herder's essays were mentioned by them and can be found in the footnotes of this edition. Their list may be supplemented by two English works of the eighteenth century: Lord Monboddo [James Burnett], *Of the Origin and Progress of Language* (1773–92); and Adam Smith, "Considerations Concerning the First Formation of Language," appended to the second edition of *Theory of Moral Sentiments* (1759).

The nineteenth-century output of original works on the subject remained profuse. A partial list of contributing authors includes L. Geiger (1869), J. Grimm (1852), A. Marty (1875), L. Noiré (1877), P. Regnaud (1887), E. Renan (1859), H. Steinthal (1851), E. B. Taylor (1866).

The English translation here presented of Rousseau's essay *On the Origin of Languages* is based on the French text found in *Oeuvres complètes de J. J. Rousseau,* tome troisième (Paris: Furne, 1852). Other French editions include Charles Porset, ed., *Jean-Jacques Rousseau, Essai sur l'origine des langues où il est parlé de la mélodie et de l'imitation musicale* (Bordeaux: Ducros, 1968); and Bernard Gagnebin and Marcel Raymond, eds., *Oeuvres complètes* (Paris: Gallimard, Bibliothèque de la Pléiade 11, 1959–69).

The English translation here presented of Herder's essay *On the Origin of Language* is based on the German text found in *Herders Sämmtliche Werke,* volume V, edited by Bernard Suphan, (Berlin, 1891). The translator has, however, made liberal use of his assumed right to consult all accessible variants and to decide from case to case which one to follow in the interest of clarity.

Jean-Jacques Rousseau

Title

ESSAY
on the
ORIGIN OF LANGUAGES
which treats of
MELODY AND
MUSICAL IMITATION

Translated by
JOHN H. MORAN

CONTENTS

CHAPTER ONE

On the Various Means of Communicating Our Thoughts

Speech distinguishes man among the animals; language distinguishes nations from each other; one does not know where a man comes from until he has spoken. Out of usage and necessity, each learns the language of his own country. But what determines that this language is that of his country and not of another? In order to tell, it is necessary to go back to some principle that belongs to the locality itself and antedates its customs, for speech, being the first social institution, owes its form to natural causes alone.

As soon as one man was recognized by another as a sentient, thinking being similar to himself, the desire or need to communicate his feelings and thoughts made him seek the means to do so. Such means can be derived only from the senses, the only instruments through which one man can act upon another. Hence the institution of sensate signs for the expression of thought. The inventors of language did not proceed rationally in this way; rather their instinct suggested the consequence to them.

Generally, the means by which we can act on the

5

senses of others are restricted to two: that is, movement
and voice. The action of movement is immediate through
touching, or mediate through gesture. The first can function only within arm's length, while the other extends as
far as the visual ray. Thus vision and hearing are the
only passive organs of language among distinct individuals.

Although the language of gesture and spoken language
are equally natural, still the first is easier and depends
less upon conventions. For more things affect our eyes
than our ears. Also, visual forms are more varied than
sounds, and more expressive, saying more in less time.
Love, it is said, was the inventor of drawing. It might
also have invented speech, though less happily. Not being
very well pleased with it, it disdains it; it has livelier
ways of expressing itself. How she could say things to
her beloved, who traced his shadow with such pleasure!
What sounds might she use to work such magic?

Our gestures merely indicate our natural unrest. It is
not of those that I wish to speak. Only Europeans gesticulate when speaking; one might say that all their power
of speech is in their arms. Their lungs are powerful too,
but to nearly no avail. Where a Frenchman would strain
and torture his body, emitting a great verbal torrent,
a Turk will momentarily remove his pipe from his mouth
to utter a few words softly, crushing one with a single
sentence.

Since learning to gesticulate, we have forgotten the art
of pantomime, for the same reason that with all our
beautiful systems of grammar we no longer understand
the symbols of the Egyptians. What the ancients said in
the liveliest way, they did not express in words but by
means of signs. They did not say it, they showed it.

Consider ancient history; it is full of such ways of ap-
pealing to the eye, each of them more effective than all

the discourse that might have replaced it. An object held up before speaking will arouse the imagination, excite curiosity, hold the mind in suspense, in expectation of what will be said. I have noticed that Italians and Provençals, among whom gesture ordinarily precedes discourse, use this as a way of drawing attention and of pleasing their listeners. But in the most vigorous language, everything is said symbolically, before one actually speaks. Tarquin, or Thrasybulus lopping off poppies; Alexander applying his seal to the mouth of his favorite; Diogenes promenading in front of Zeno: do they not speak more effectively than with words? What verbal circumlocution would express the same idea as well? Darius, engaged with his army in Scythia, receives from the King of Scythia a frog, a bird, a mouse, and five arrows. The herald makes the presentation in silence and departs. That terrible harangue was understood; and Darius returned to his own country as quickly as he could. Substitute a letter for this sign: the more menacing it is, the less frightening will it be. It will be no more than a boast, which would draw merely a smile from Darius.

When the Levite of Ephraim wanted to avenge the death of his wife, he wrote nothing to the tribes of Israel, but divided her body into twelve sections which he sent to them. At this horrible sight they rushed to arms, crying with one voice: *Never has such a thing happened in Israel, from the time of our fathers' going out of Egypt, down to the present day!* And the tribe of Benjamin was exterminated.[1] In our day, this affair, recounted in court pleadings and discussions, perhaps in jest, would be dragged out until this most horrible of crimes would in the end have remained unpunished. King Saul, returning

---

[1] There remained only 600 men, with no women or children.

from the fields, similarly dismembered his plow oxen, thus using a similar sign to make Israel march to the aid of the city of Jabes. The Jewish prophets and the Greek lawgivers, by frequently presenting sensate objects to the people, spoke to them more effectively through these objects than they would have by means of lengthy discourse. The way the Athenaeum yields when the orator Hyperides made them acquit the courtesan Phryne, without alleging a single word in her defense, is another mute eloquence, the effects of which are not unusual in any age.

Thus one speaks more effectively to the eye than to the ear. There is no one who does not feel the truth of Horace's judgment in this regard. Clearly the most eloquent speeches are those containing the most imagery; and sounds are never more forceful than when they produce the effects of colors.

But when it is a question of stirring the heart and inflaming the passions, it is an altogether different matter. The successive impressions of discourse, which strike a redoubled blow, produce a different feeling from that of the continuous presence of the same object, which can be taken in at a single glance. Imagine someone in a painful situation that is fully known; as you watch the afflicted person, you are not likely to weep. But give him time to tell you what he feels and soon you will burst into tears. It is solely in this way that the scenes of a tragedy produce their effect.[2]

Pantomime without discourse will leave you nearly tranquil; discourse without gestures will wring tears

---

[2] I have said elsewhere why feigned misfortunes touch us more than real ones. There is a type that weeps at a tragedy, yet has never had any pity for the suffering. The invention of theater is remarkable for inflating our pride with all the virtues in which we are entirely lacking.

from you. The passions have their gestures, but they
also have their accents; and these accents, which thrill
us, these tones of voice that cannot fail to be heard,
penetrate to the very depths of the heart, carrying there
the emotions they wring from us, forcing us in spite of
ourselves to feel what we hear. We conclude that while
visible signs can render a more exact imitation, sounds
more effectively arouse interest.

This leads me to think that if the only needs we ever
experienced were physical, we should most likely never
have been able to speak; we would fully express our
meanings by the language of gesture alone. We would
have been able to establish societies little different from
those we have, or such as would have been better able
to achieve their goals. We would have been able to in-
stitute laws, to choose leaders, to invent arts, to establish
commerce, and to do, in a word, almost as many things
as we do with the help of speech. Without fear of
jealousy, the secrets of oriental gallantry are passed across
the more strictly guarded harems in the epistolary
language of salaams.[3] The mutes of great nobles understand each other, and understand everything that is said
to them by means of signs, just as well as one can understand anything said in discourse. M. Pereyra and those
like him who not only consider that mutes speak, but
claim to understand what they are saying, had to learn
another language, as complicated as our own, in order
to understand them.

Chardin says that in India, traders would take each
other by the hand, varying their grip in a way that no
one could see, thus transacting all their business pub-

---

[3] Many very common items, such as an orange, a ribbon, charcoal,
etc., are used as salaams, the sending of which has a meaning
known to all the lovers of the country in which this language is
used.

licly yet secretly, without a single word being uttered. If these traders had been blind, deaf, and mute, this would not hinder their understanding of each other; which shows that of the two senses by which we act, one alone will suffice to form a language.

It appears again, by the same observations, that the invention of the art of communicating our ideas depends less upon the organs we use in such communication than it does upon a power proper to man, according to which he uses his organs in this way, and which, if he lacked these, would lead him to use others to the same end. Give man a structure [organically] as crude as you please: doubtless he will acquire fewer ideas, but if only he has some means of contact with his fellow men, by means of which one can act and another can sense, he will finally succeed in communicating whatever ideas he might have.

Animals have a more than adequate structure for such communication, but none of them has ever made use of it. This seems to me a quite characteristic difference. That those animals which live and work in common, such as beavers, ants, bees, have some natural language for communicating among themselves, I would not question. Still, the speech of beavers and ants is apparently by gesture; i.e., it is only visual. If so, such languages are natural, not acquired. The animals that speak them possess them a-borning: they all have them, and they are everywhere the same. They are entirely unchanging and make not the slightest progress. Conventional language is characteristic of man alone. That is why man makes progress, whether for good or ill, and animals do not. That single distinction would seem to be far-reaching. It is said to be explicable by organic differences. I would be curious to witness this explanation.

CHAPTER TWO

That the First Invention of Speech Is Due Not to Need but Passion

It seems then that need dictated the first gestures, while the passions stimulated the first words. By pursuing the course of the facts with these distinctions we may be able to see the question of the origin of language in an entirely new light. The genesis of oriental languages, the oldest known, absolutely refutes the assumption of a didactic progression in their development. These languages are not at all systematic or rational. They are vital and figurative. The language of the first men is represented to us as the tongues of geometers, but we see that they were the tongues of poets.

And so it had to be. One does not begin by reasoning, but by feeling. It is suggested that men invented speech to express their needs: an opinion which seems to me untenable. The natural effect of the first needs was to separate men, and not to reunite them. It must have been that way, because the species spread out and the earth was promptly populated. Otherwise mankind would have been crammed into a small area of the world, and the rest would have remained uninhabited.

From this alone it follows clearly that the origin of languages is not at all due to people's first needs. It would be absurd to suppose that the means of uniting them derived from the cause of their separation. Whence then this origin? From moral needs, passions. All the passions tend to bring people back together again, but the necessity of seeking a livelihood forces them apart. It is neither hunger nor thirst but love, hatred, pity, anger, which drew from them the first words. Fruit does not disappear from our hands. One can take nourishment without speaking. One stalks in silence the prey on which one would feast. But for moving a young heart, or repelling an unjust aggressor, nature dictates accents, cries, lamentations. There we have the invention of the most ancient words; and that is why the first languages were singable and passionate before they became simple and methodical. All of this is not true without qualification, but I shall return to it in the sequel.

CHAPTER THREE

That the First Language Had To Be Figurative

As man's first motives for speaking were of the passions, his first expressions were tropes. Figurative language was the first to be born. Proper meaning was discovered last. One calls things by their true name only when one sees them in their true form. At first only poetry was spoken; there was no hint of reasoning until much later.

However, I feel the reader stopping me at this point

to ask how an expression can be figurative before it has a proper meaning, since the figure consists only of a transference of meaning. I agree with that. But, in order to understand what I mean, it is necessary to substitute the idea that the passion presents to us for the word that we transpose. For one does not only transpose words; one also transposes ideas. Otherwise figurative language would signify nothing. I shall reply then with an example.

Upon meeting others, a savage man will initially be frightened. Because of his fear he sees the others as bigger and stronger than himself. He calls them *giants.* After many experiences, he recognizes that these so-called giants are neither bigger nor stronger than he. Their stature does not approach the idea he had initially attached to the word giant. So he invents another name common to them and to him, such as the name *man,* for example, and leaves *giant* to the fictitious object that had impressed him during his illusion. That is how the figurative word is born before the literal word, when our gaze is held in passionate fascination; and how it is that the first idea it conveys to us is not that of the truth.

What I have said of words and names presents no difficulty relative to the forms of phrases. The illusory image presented by passion is the first to appear, and the language that corresponded to it was also the first invented. It subsequently became metaphorical when the enlightened spirit, recognizing its first error, used the expressions only with those passions that had produced them.

CHAPTER FOUR

On the Distinctive Characteristics of the First Language and the Changes It Had To Undergo

Simple sounds emerge naturally from the throat; and the mouth is naturally more or less open. But the modifications of the tongue and palate, which produce articulation, require attention and practice. One does not make them at all without willing to make them. All children need to learn them, and some do not succeed easily. In all tongues, the liveliest exclamations are inarticulate. Cries and groans are simple sounds. Mutes, which is to say the deaf, can make only inarticulate sounds. Father Lamy thinks that if God had not taught men to speak, they would never have learned by themselves. There are only a small number of articulations; there are infinitely many sounds, and the accents that distinguish them can be equally numerous. All the musical notes are just so many accents. True, we have only three or four in speech. The Chinese have many more; but on the other hand, they have fewer consonants. To these possible combinations, add those of tense and number, and you have not only more words, but more distinct syllables than even the richest tongue requires.

I do not doubt that independent of vocabulary and syntax, the first tongue, if it still existed, would retain the original characteristics that would distinguish it from all others. Not only would all the forms of this tongue have to be in images, feelings, and figures, but even in its mechanical part it would have to correspond to its initial object, presenting to the senses as well as to the understanding the almost inevitable impression of the feeling that it seeks to communicate.

Since natural sounds are inarticulate, words have few articulations. Interposing some consonants to fill the gaps between vowels would suffice to make them fluid and easy to pronounce. On the other hand, the sounds would be very varied, and the diversity of accents for each sound would further multiply them. Quantity and rhythm would account for still further combinations. Since sounds, accents, and number, which are natural, would leave little to articulation, which is conventional, it would be sung rather than spoken. Most of the root words would be imitative sounds or accents of passion, or effects of sense objects. It would contain many onomatopoeic expressions.

This language would have many synonyms for expressing the same thing according to various relationships.[1] It would have few adverbs and abstract names for expressing these same relationships. It would have many augmentatives, diminutives, composite words, expletive particles to indicate the cadence of sentences and fullness of phrases. It would have many irregularities and anomalies. It would deemphasize grammatical analogy for euphony, number, harmony, and beauty of sounds. Instead of arguments, it would have aphorisms. It would persuade without convincing, and would represent without reasoning. It would resemble Chinese in certain respects, Greek and Arabic in others. If you understand

---

[1] It is said that the Arabs have more than a thousand different words for *camel* and more than a hundred for *sword,* etc.

these ideas in all their ramifications, you will find that Plato's *Cratylus* is not as ridiculous as it appears to be.*

CHAPTER FIVE

On Script

Anyone who studies the history and progress of the tongues will see that the more the words become monotonous, the more the consonants multiply; that, as accents fall into disuse and quantities are neutralized, they are replaced by grammatical combinations and new articulations. But only the pressure of time brings these changes about. To the degree that needs multiply, that affairs become complicated, that light is shed, language changes its character. It becomes more regular and less passionate. It substitutes ideas for feelings. It no longer speaks to the heart but to reason. Similarly, accent diminishes, articulation increases. Language becomes more exact and clearer, but more prolix, duller and colder. This progression seems to me entirely natural.

Another way of comparing languages and determining their relative antiquity is to consider their script, and reason inversely from the degree of perfection of this art. The cruder the writing, the more ancient the lan-

---

* That is, in treating of whether (etymologically compound) names are *true,* on the basis of the supposed immediate reference of their elementary component names.—Tr.

guage. The primitive way of writing was not to represent sounds, but objects themselves whether directly, as with the Mexicans, or by allegorical imagery, or as the Egyptians did in still other ways. This stage corresponds to passionate language, and already supposes some society and some needs to which the passions have given birth.

The second way is to represent words and propositions by conventional characters. That can be done only when the language is completely formed and an entire people is united by common laws; for this already presupposes a twofold convention. Such is the writing of Chinese; it truly represents sounds and speaks to the eyes.

The third is to break down the speaking voice into a given number of elementary parts, either vocal or articulate, with which one can form all the words and syllables imaginable. This way of writing, which is ours, must have been invented by commercial peoples who, in traveling to various countries, had to speak various languages, which would have impelled them to invent characters that could be common to all of them. This is not exactly to represent speech, but to analyze it.

These three ways of writing correspond almost exactly to three different stages according to which one can consider men gathered into a nation. The depicting of objects is appropriate to a savage people; signs of words and of propositions, to a barbaric people, and the alphabet to civilized peoples [*peuples policés*]. One need not think that this latter device is proof of the great antiquity of the people who invented it. On the contrary, those who invented it probably did so in order to facilitate communication with other people who spoke other languages as old as their own, if not older. The same cannot be said of the two other methods. I grant, however, that if one sticks to history and to known facts, alphabetical writing appears to go back as far as any other. But it is not surprising that we have no record of times when there was no writing.

It is not very likely that the first people to resolve language into elementary signs made very exact divisions initially. When it later became clear to them that their analysis was insufficient, some, such as the Greeks, made additions to their alphabet. Others were content to vary the meaning or the sound of an expression by various combinations and positions. The inscriptions on the ruins of Tchelminar, which Chardin has deciphered for us, appear to have been written in that way. There are only two distinct figures or characters,[1] but of varied sizes and placed in various positions, for various meanings. This unknown language of almost startling antiquity is, nonetheless, well formed, judging from the perfection of the arts as indicated in the beauty of the characters[2]

---

[1] Chardin says it is astonishing that two figures can do as much as all our letters. But I see nothing astonishing in this, since the letters of our alphabet, which number twenty-three, are nevertheless composed of only two lines, the straight and the circular. That is, with C and I, one can form all the letters that enter into any of our words.

[2] "These characters are quite beautiful in appearance, not at all confused or barbarous. The letters are said to have been gilded, for there is still some gilt on them, especially the capitals, which still look golden. It is certainly remarkable that the atmosphere has been unable to wear away this gilding in so many centuries. However, it is not remarkable that no scholar has ever understood anything written in this language, since it is in no way like any language known to us. All the systems of writing known today, except Chinese, have many affinities to each other, and appear to derive from the same source. Most remarkable in this connection are the Guebres, the remnants of ancient Persia. For they preserved and perpetuated the religion, still not only are they as unfamiliar with these characters as we, but their own characters resemble them no more than ours do. From this it follows either that it is a cabalist character, which is improbable, since it is the natural and usual character, used throughout the edifice, and since no other is used in

and the admirable monuments on which these inscriptions were found. I do not know why there is so little discussion about these amazing ruins. When I read Chardin's description of them, I am as it were transported to another world. It all seems to me intensely thought-provoking.

The art of writing does not at all depend upon that of speaking. It derives from needs of a different kind which develop earlier or later according to circumstances entirely independent of the duration of the people, and which might never have occurred in very old nations. Who knows how long the Egyptians had no other system of writing than hieroglyphics. That such a system is sufficient for a civilized people is proved by the example of the Mexicans, whose system is even less practical.

In comparing the Coptic alphabet to the Syrian or Phoenician, it can easily be seen that the one derives from the other. And it would not be surprising that the latter was the original, nor that the more modern people has taught the more ancient in this way. It is also clear that the Greek alphabet derives from the Phoenician, and is indebted to it. Whether Cadmus or someone else brought it from Phoenicia, it seems certain that the Greeks did not seek it out, but that the Phoenicians themselves brought it to them. For they are the first and almost the only[3] people of Asia or Africa who originated in Europe, and they came to the Greeks much earlier than the Greeks went to them: which does not necessarily

the same way; or else it is of such great antiquity that we should hardly dare to speak it." In effect, Chardin has made the assumption in this passage that from the time of Cyrus and the wise men, these characters were already forgotten, as little known as today. [The Rosetta Stone was discovered in 1799, twenty years after Rousseau's death.—Tr.]

[3] I consider the Carthaginians Phoenicians, since Carthage was a colony of Tyre.

prove that the Greeks were not as ancient as the people of Phoenicia.

At first they adopted not only the characters of the Phoenicians, but also the direction of their lines from right to left. Later it occurred to them to proceed as the plowman, that is, writing alternately from left to right and right to left.[4] Finally, they wrote according to our present practice of starting each line from left to right. This development is quite natural. Writing in the furrow fashion is undoubtedly the most comfortable to read. I am even surprised that it did not become the established practice with printing; but, being difficult to write manually, it had to be abandoned as manuscripts multiplied.

But though the Greek alphabet derives from the Phoenician, it does not follow at all that the Greek language derives from the Phoenician. One of these propositions has no dependence upon the other; and it seems the Greek language was already quite ancient at a time when the art of writing was still very primitive in Greece. Until the siege of Troy, the Greek alphabet had at most sixteen letters. There is a tradition that Palamedes added four, and Simonides the other four, all within a short time. On the other hand, Latin, a more modern language, had a complete alphabet almost from the beginning. But the early Romans made scant use of it, since they began so late to record their history, and would merely mark off the lustrums with nail heads.

Besides, there is no absolutely determinate number of letters, or elements of speech. The number may vary according to the language, and according to the various modifications of voice, and consonants. Those who recognize only five vowels are quite deceived: the Greeks had

---

[4] See Pausanias, *Arcadia*. The Latins originally wrote in the same way; and from that, according to Marius Victorinus, came the word *versus*.

seven written vowels, the first Romans had six.[5] The gentlemen of Port-Royal count ten, M. Duclos, seventeen. And I do not doubt that many more could be distinguished, if custom had made the ear more sensitive and the mouth more practiced in the various modifications of which they are capable. Depending on the refinement of the voice, there will be a greater or a lesser difference between the acute *a* and the grave *o*, between the *i* and the open *e*, etc. Anyone can check this by making the transition from one vowel sound to another, through the continuous intermediate shadings; for one can stop at any point, more or less fixing upon a given nuance, and mark it with a particular character, according as the force of habit makes it more or less perceptible. And this habit depends upon the kinds of sounds occurring in the language, according to which the voice develops imperceptibly. Much the same can be said of the articulated letters or consonants. But most countries have not done so. They have adopted each other's alphabets, and represented very dissimilar sounds and articulations by the same characters. Thus, unless one is extremely well versed in a foreign language, one always gives a ridiculous reading of those of its expressions that are spelled the same as expressions in one's own language.

Writing, which would seem to crystallize language, is precisely what alters it. It changes not the words but the spirit, substituting exactitude for expressiveness. Feelings are expressed in speaking, ideas in writing. In writing, one is forced to use all the words according to their conventional meaning. But in speaking, one varies the

---

[5] *"Vocales quas graece septem, Romulus sex, usus posterior quinque commemorat, Y velut graeca rejecta.* Mart. Capel., *lib.* iii. ["The Greek language has seven vowels, that of Romulus has six, and later practice notes five, as 'Y' is a throwback to Greek." Martianus Mineus Felix Capella (c. A.D. 400-439), *Satyricon*, Bk. iii.]

meanings by varying one's tone of voice, determining them as one pleases. Being less constrained to clarity, one can be more forceful. And it is not possible for a language that is written, to retain its vitality as long as one that is only spoken. Words [*voix*], not sounds [*sons*], are written. Yet, in an inflected language, these are the sounds, the accents, and all sorts of modulations that are the main source of energy for a language, and that make a given phrase, otherwise quite ordinary, uniquely appropriate. The means used to overcome this weakness tend to make written language rather elaborately prolix; and many books written in discourse will enervate the language.[6]

To say everything as one would write it would be merely to read aloud.

---

[6] Punctuation, which does not have this defect, would be the best of such means if it were more complete. Why, for example, do we not have a vocative mark? The question mark, which we have, would be much less necessary, since a question is recognizable from its structure alone, at least in our language. *Venez vous* and *vous venez* are not the same. But how is one to distinguish, in writing, between a man one mentions and a man one addresses. There really is an equivocation which would be eliminated by a vocative mark. The same equivocation is found in irony, when it is not made manifest by accent.

CHAPTER SIX

Whether It Is Likely that Homer Knew How To Write

Whatever we are told about the invention of the Greek alphabet, I believe it is much more modern than it is made out to be. I base this opinion principally on the character of the language. It has often occurred to me in skeptical moments not only that Homer knew how to write, but that he wrote in the manner of his time. I am very sorry if this doubt is formally contradicted by the story of Bellerophon in the *Iliad.*° But since I share with Fr. Harduin the misfortune of being a bit stubborn in my paradoxes, if I were less ignorant I might well try to extend my doubting to this very story, arguing that it had been uncritically interpolated by the compilers of Homer. What is more, there are few traces of the art in the remainder of the *Iliad.* But I venture to suggest that the whole *Odyssey* is just a tissue of inanities and stupidities that would be dissolved by changing a letter or two. Instead, the poem is made reasonable and fairly continuous, by presuming that these heroes did not know how to write. Had the *Iliad* been written, it would have been sung much less. Rhapsodies would have been less in demand, and less numerous. What other poet, besides

---

° Bk. vi, especially lines 165-75, is the only passage in Homer that suggests knowledge of the art of writing.—Tr.

Tasso of Venice, has been sung so much? Again, Tasso is sung by none other than the Gondoliers, who are not great readers. Again, the diversity of dialects used by Homer is strong presumptive evidence. Dialects tend to be distinguished by oral speech, while writing tends to assimilate and merge them; they all tend imperceptibly to correspond to a common pattern. The more a people read and learn, the more are its dialects obliterated, and finally they remain only as a form of slang among people who read little and do not write at all.

But these two poems are later than the siege of Troy, and it is hardly obvious that the Greeks who made the siege knew how to write, or that the poet who sang of it did not know. For a long time these poems were written only in men's memories. Somewhat later they were laboriously collected in writing. That was when Greece began to abound in books and written poetry, whereby all the charm of Homer could be experienced by comparison. Other poets had written; Homer alone had sung. And people have always listened in rapture to these songs, even when Europe has been overrun by barbarians who try to judge what they are incapable of experiencing.

CHAPTER SEVEN

On Modern Prosody

We have no idea of a sonorous and harmonious language, spoken as much according to sounds as it is according to words. It is mistaken to think that accent marks can make up for oral intonation. One invents accent signs [*accens*] only when intonation [*l'accent*] has already been lost.[1]

Furthermore, we think we have accents in our language, and we have none at all. Our supposed accents are only vowels, or signs of quantity. They do not indicate any distinctions among sounds. Proof of this is the fact that these accents all come about either through differences of tense or through movements of the lips, of the tongue or of the palate, which produce the various tones of voice, and not by changes in the glottis which produce the various sounds. Thus when our circumflex is not used to indicate a simple sound, either it indicates a long syllable or nothing. Now let us see what it would be for the Greeks.

> Denis of Halicarnassus says that the raising of tone indicated by the acute accent and the lowering for the grave would be a fifth. Thus the prosodic accent would also be musical, especially the circumflex, where the voice, having risen by a fifth, drops by another fifth, on the same syllable.[2]

It is clear enough from this and related passages that M. Duclos completely overlooks musical accent in our language, noting only the vocal and prosodic accents. In addition there are orthographic accents, for which there are no corresponding vocal distinctions, either of sounds or of quantity. They sometimes indicate the omission of a letter, as does the circumflex, and sometimes determine the meaning of a monosyllable, as the so-called *accent grave* which distinguishes *où* as an adverb from *ou* as a disjunctive particle, and *à* taken as an article from *a* taken as a verb. This accent makes only a visual

---

[1] See note at end of chapter.
[2] M. Duclos, *Remarques sur la grammaire générale raisonnée*, p. 50.

difference in these monosyllables; it does not affect their pronounciation.[3]

Thus the usual French definition of accent does not accord with any of the accents of their language. I am confident, however, that some of their grammarians, having prejudged that accent marks indicate a raising or lowering of the voice, are nonetheless amazed at the resulting paradox. And, ignoring experience, they propose to produce, by movements of the glottis, the very accents that are produced solely by varying the opening of the mouth and the position of the tongue. But what I want to suggest to them would be confirmed by experience and would incontrovertibly establish my point.

Attune your voice exactly to some musical instrument, and pronounce accordingly all the most variously accented French words you can muster. As there is no question here of oratorical, but only grammatical accent, the sequence of these words need not make sense. As you pronounce the words in this way, observe whether you do not indicate all the accents just as clearly and distinctly without varying the sound as if you pronounced them with the normal variations in tone of voice. But presumably, and I say incontestably, since you expressed all the accents in the same tone, they do not indicate any difference of sounds. I think that is indisputable.

Any language, in which the same words can be set to several different melodies, has no determinate musical accent. If the accent were definite, then the melody would be too. Whenever the tune is arbitrary, accent counts for nothing.

---

[3] Undoubtedly the Italians distinguish by the same accent, between, for example, the verb *è* and the conjunction *e*; but the first is also aurally distinguished by a harder, more emphatic sound, which makes it a vocal accent: an observation Buonmattei was wrong in not making.

This is more or less true of all modern European languages, including Italian. Considered in itself, the Italian language is no more musical than is French. The difference is merely that the one lends itself to music and the other does not.

All this tends to confirm the principle that literary languages are naturally bound to undergo changes of character, and to lose in power what they gain in clarity; that the more stress on perfecting of grammar and logic, the faster these changes occur. All that is needed for quickly rendering a language cold and monotonous, is to establish academies among the people who speak it.

Derivative languages are marked by a discrepancy between orthography and pronunciation. The older and more original a language is, the less arbitrary its pronunciation, and consequently, the less complicated the signs for indicating that pronunciation. According to M. Duclos, "all the ancient prosodic signs supposed a quite fixed function, not yet bowing to usage." I would add that they substituted for it. The ancient Hebrews had neither punctuation nor accent marks; they did not even have vowels. When other peoples wanted to take the trouble to speak Hebrew and the Jews to speak other languages, their own lost its accent. It needed punctuation marks, signs to regulate it. And that did much more to retain the meaning of the words than the pronunciation of the language. Jews speaking Hebrew today would not be understood by their ancestors.

To know English one must learn it twice: first, to read it, and second to speak it. If a foreigner looks at a book from which an Englishman is reading aloud, the foreigner will not perceive any connection between what he sees and what he hears the Englishman say. Why is that? Because England has been successively conquered by various peoples and, while their words have always been written in the same way, the way of pronouncing them has often changed. There is a great deal of difference between the signs that determine the meaning of writing and those that govern pronunciation. It would be easy to construct a language consisting solely of consonants, which could be written clearly but not spoken. Algebra has something of such a language. When the orthography of a language is clearer than its pronunciation, this is a sign that it is written more than it is spoken. This may have been true of the scholarly language of the Egyptians; as is the case for us with the dead languages. In those burdened with useless consonants, writing seems to have preceded speech: and who would doubt that such is the case with Polish? If it is, then Polish must be the coldest of all languages.

NOTE

Some scholars propose, against the consensus and against the tired old evidence drawn from all the ancient manuscripts, that the Greeks had known and used what are called accent marks. They base this opinion on the two passages which I am going to transcribe in juxtaposition, so the reader can judge their true meaning. Here is the first, taken from Cicero's *Treatise on the Orator*, Bk. III, No. 44:

"*Hanc diligentiam subsequitur modus etiam et forma verborum, quod jam vereor ne hic Catulo videatur esse puerile. Versus enim veteres illi in hac soluta oratione propemodum, hoc est, numeros quosdam nobis esse adhibendos putaverunt. Interspirationis enim non defatigationis nostrae, neque librariorum notis, sed verborum et sententiarum modo, interpunctas clausulas in orationibus esse voluerunt; idque princeps Isocrates instituisse fertur, ut inconditam antiquorumdicendi consuetudinem, delectationis atque aurium causa (quem admodum scribit discipulus ejus Naucrates), numeris adstringeret.*

"*Namque haec duo musici, qui erant quondam idem poetae, machinati ad voluptatem sunt, versum atque cantum, eut et verborum numero, et vocum modo, delectatione vincerent aurium sati-*

*etatem. Haec igitur duo, vocis dico moderationem, et verborum
conclusionem, quod orationis severitas pati possit, a poetica ad elo-
quentiam traducenda duxerunt."*

["After attention to this matter there is still the consideration of
rhythm and the shape of words, a point which I am afraid Catulus
here may view as childish; for the old masters held that in this
prose style we are free to use what hardly differs from verse, that is,
certain definite rhythms. For they thought that in speeches, the
close of the period should come not when we are tired but where
we can take a breath, and to be marked not by the punctuation of
the copyists, but by the nature of the words and of the thoughts;
and Isocrates is said to have started the practice of tightening up the
loose style of ancient times (so his pupil Naucrates writes) by
means of rhythm, designed to give pleasure to the ear.

"For two means of giving pleasure were devised by the musicians, who in the old days were also the poets: verse and melody,
with the intention of overcoming satiety in the listener by pleasing
the ear with the rhythm of the words and the mode of the notes.
These two things, therefore, I mean the modulation of the voice
and the arrangement of words in periods, they thought proper to
transfer from poetry to rhetoric, so far as was compatible with the
severe character of oratory."]

Here is the second, taken from Isidore's Origins, Book I,
Chapter XX:

*"Praeterea quaedam sententiarum notae apud celeberrimos
auctores fuerunt, quasque antiqui ad distinctionem scripturarum
carminibus et historiis apposuerunt. Nota est figura propria in lit-
terae modum posita, ad demonstrandum unamquamque verbi sen-
tentiarumque ac versuum rationem. Notae autem versibus apponun-
tur numero XXVI, quae sunt nominibus infra scriptis, etc."*

["Besides, there were certain of the meanings of a mark among
the most famous authors, which also were used by the ancients for
written distinctions in song and story. A mark is a definite character, placed in the manner of a letter, to indicate the meaning of
each word and also the versification. But marks, 26 in number,
which are written below names, etc., are put to verses."]

To me this shows that in Cicero's time, good copyists made a
practice of separating words, and of using signs equivalent to our
punctuation marks. I see here the invention of number and of prose
declamation attributed again to Isocrates. But I do not see anything here of all the written accent signs. And if I did find them,
one could only conclude what I do not dispute, and what goes right
back to my principles, namely, that when the Romans began to

study Greek, the copyists invented accent marks, aspiration marks, and marks of prosody, to indicate their pronunciation. But by no means does it follow that these signs were in use among the Greeks, who would not need them.

CHAPTER EIGHT

General and Local Difference in the Origin of Languages

All that I have said so far applies to primitive tongues in general, and to such development as is due merely to the passage of time. But it does not explain either their origin or their differences. The principal cause that distinguishes them is local, deriving from the various climates in which they are born, and the way in which they take form. It is necessary to go back to this cause in order to understand the general and characteristic differences between the tongues of the south and those of the north. The great shortcoming of Europeans is always to philosophize on the origins of things exclusively in terms of what happens within their own milieu. They never fail to show us primitive men inhabiting a barren and harsh world, dying of cold and hunger, desperate for shelter and clothing, with nothing in sight but Europe's ice and snow. But they fail to realize that, just like all life, the human race originated in warm climes, and that on two-thirds of the globe, winter is hardly known. When one wants to study men, one must consider those around one. But to study man, one must extend the range of one's vision. One must first observe the differences in order to discover the properties.

The human race, born in warm lands, spread itself into cold areas where it multiplied, and then coursed back into the warm lands. From this action and reaction come the revolutions of the earth and the continual agitation of its inhabitants. Let us try to follow the order of nature in our investigations. I shall enter now upon a long digression on a subject so hackneyed it is trivial, but one to which it is nonetheless always necessary to return, in order to find the origin of human institutions.

CHAPTER NINE

Formation of the Southern Languages

In primitive times[1] the sparse human population had no more social structure than the family, no laws but those of nature, no language but that of gesture and some inarticulate sounds.[2] They were not bound by any idea

---

[1] I consider primitive the period of time from the dispersion of men to any period of the human race that might be taken as determining an epoch.

[2] Genuine languages are not at all of domestic origin. They can be established only under a more general, more durable agreement. The American savages hardly speak at all except outside their homes. Each keeps silent in his hut, speaking to his family by signs. And these signs are used infrequently, for a savage is less disquieted, less impatient than a European; he has fewer needs and he is careful to meet them himself.

of common brotherhood and, having no rule but that of force, they believed themselves each other's enemies. This belief was due to their weakness and ignorance. Knowing nothing, they feared everything. They attacked in self-defense. An individual isolated on the face of the earth, at the mercy of mankind, is bound to be a ferocious animal. He would be ready to do unto others all the evil that he feared from them. Fear and weakness are the sources of cruelty.

We develop social feeling only as we become enlightened. Although pity is native to the human heart, it would remain eternally quiescent unless it were activated by imagination. How are we moved to pity? By getting outside ourselves and identifying with a being who suffers. We suffer only as much as we believe him to suffer. It is not in ourselves, but in him that we suffer. It is clear that such transport supposes a great deal of acquired knowledge. How am I to imagine ills of which I have no idea? How would I suffer in seeing another suffer, if I know not what he is suffering, if I am ignorant of what he and I have in common. He who has never been reflective is incapable of being merciful or just or pitying. He is just as incapable of being malicious and vindictive. He who imagines nothing is aware only of himself; he is isolated in the midst of mankind.

Reflection is born of the comparison of ideas, and it is the plurality of ideas that leads to their comparison. One who is aware of only a single object has no basis for comparison. And those whose experience remains confined to the narrow range of their childhood also are incapable of such comparisons. Long familiarity deprives them of the attention requisite for such examination. But to the degree that something strikes us as novel, we want to know it. We seek rapport with those we know. Thus we come to ponder what is before our faces, and experience of the strange leads us to examine the familiar.

Apply these thoughts to primitive men and you see the reason for their barbarity. Never having seen anything beyond their own immediate milieu, they did not even understand that; they did not understand themselves. They had the concept of a father, a son, a brother, but not that of a man. Their hut contained all of their fellow men. Stranger, beast, monster: these were all one to them. Apart from themselves and their family, the whole universe would count as nothing to them.

This accounts for the apparent contradictions seen in the fathers of nations: so natural, and so inhuman; such ferocious behavior and such tender hearts; so much love for their families and such antipathy to their species. All their feelings, being concentrated on those near them, would be more intense. Everyone they knew would be dear to them; enemies the rest of the world, whom they did not see at all, of whom they were ignorant. They hated only those with whom they could not be acquainted.

These barbaric times were a golden age, not because men were united, but because they were separated. Each, it is said, considered himself master of all. That might be, but none of them knew or wanted to control anyone beyond those who were at hand. His needs, far from drawing him closer to his fellows, drove him from them. If you wish, men would attack each other when they met, but they rarely met. A state of war prevailed universally, and the entire earth was at peace.

The first men were hunters or shepherds, and not tillers of the soil; herdsmen, not men of the fields. Before the ownership of it was divided, no one thought to cultivate land. Agriculture is an art that requires tools. Sowing for harvest is a precaution which presupposes foresight. Man in society seeks to extend himself, while man in isolation retrenches. Beyond the range of his own vision or the reach of his arm, there are for him neither rights nor property. When Cyclops has rolled the stone in front of his cave, he and his herds are secure. But who would guard the crops of him for whom the laws do not give protection?

I am told that Cain was a farmer and Noah planted grapes. Why not? They were solitaries. What did they have to fear? Besides, this does not conflict with my thesis. I have said what I understand by primitive times. In becoming a fugitive, Cain was compelled to give up agriculture, and the wandering life of Noah's descendants forced them to give it up too. The earth has to be peopled before it can be cultivated; the two cannot very well be accomplished together. During the first dispersal of the human race, until the family was instituted, and man had stable habitation, there was no more agriculture. People completely without roots will not cultivate the land. Such were the Nomads; such were the Arabs, living under tents; the Scythians in their chariots; such are the wandering Tartars, even today, and the savages of America.

Generally, among all peoples of whose origins we know, one finds the earliest ones barbarous, voracious, and carnivorous rather than agricultural and granivorous. The Greeks indicate who first tought them to till the soil, and it seems they were unacquainted with this art until very late. But when they claim that before Triptolemus they lived only on nuts they are alleging an improbability. And it is contradicted by their own history. It seems they ate flesh meat before Triptolemus, since he forbade them to do so. Besides, it does not seem that they took his prohibition very seriously.

An ox was killed to regale the guests at a Homeric feast, just as today a suckling pig is killed. When one considers that Abraham served a calf to three people, that Eumaeus had two kids roasted for Ulysses' dinner, and that Rebecca ordered as many for that of her husband [Isaac], one can judge what terrible meat-eaters were the men of those times. In order to conceive of the repasts of the ancients, the like is to be seen today only in those of the savages: I was about to say those of the English.

The first cake to be eaten was the communion of the human race. When men began to settle, they cleared a little land around their huts, more of a garden than a field. They grew a little grain which they ground between stones, and made some cakes that they cooked under ashes or over coals or on a hot stone. These were eaten only on festive occasions. This ancient custom, which was consecrated by the Jews in the Pasch, is still preserved in Persia and the West Indies, where only unleavened bread is eaten. This bread is baked in thin sheets, and is [entirely] eaten at every meal. Raised bread was made only when they needed more: for leavening does not work well with small quantities.

I know there was already a great deal of agriculture in the time of the patriarchs. It was bound to be imported early into Palestine from neighboring Egypt. The Book of Job, perhaps the most ancient book extant, speaks of the cultivation of the fields. It lists five hundred pairs of oxen among the riches of Job. The word *pair* indicates that these oxen were teamed for work. It is said explicitly that these oxen were plowing when the Shebans seized them. It can be judged how much land five hundred pairs of oxen must have plowed.

All this is true. But the ages should not be confused. The patriarchal period that we know is very remote from primitive times. Scripture lists ten intervening generations at a time when men were very long-lived. What did they do during these ten generations? We know nothing about it. Living almost without society, widely scattered, hardly speaking at all, how could they write? And given the uniformity of their isolated life, what events would they have transmitted to us?

Adam spoke, Noah spoke; but it is known that Adam was taught by God himself. In scattering, the children of Noah abandoned agriculture, and the first common tongue perished with the first society. That had happened before there was any Tower of Babel. Solitaries, isolated on desert islands, have been known to forget their own tongue. Rarely do men preserve their first language outside their own country for more than a few generations, even when they are living in society and involved in ordinary occupations.

Scattered over the vast wilderness of the world, men would relapse into the stupid barbarism in which they would be if they were born of the earth. In pursuing such natural ideas, it is easy to reconcile the authority of Scripture with the ancient monuments; and one is not reduced to treating as fables traditions as ancient as the people who have transmitted them to us.

In that brutish condition it was necessary to live. And the most active, the most robust, those who were always pushing ahead, would want to live only on fruits and hunting. Thus they became bloodthirsty hunters and despoilers; or, with time, warriors, conquerors, usurpers. History is stained with the memories of such crimes by these early kings. War and its conquests is just a kind of manhunt. Having conquered, they neglected to devour their victims: that was left to their successors.

The majority, being less active and more peaceful, settled down as soon as they could. They gathered and tamed cattle, which they rendered submissive to the human voice. To provide food for themselves, they learned to keep them and breed them; and thus pastoral life began.

Human industry begins to expand with the needs to which it gave rise. Of three modes of living possible to man, namely hunting, tending herds, and agriculture, the first develops strength, skill, and speed of body along with courage and guile of spirit. It hardens man and makes him ferocious. The land of hunters is not that of the hunt for long.[3] The process must be followed a step further, to horsemanship. The same process leads to the development of small arms: the sling, the arrow, the javelin. The pastoral art, father of repose and indolence, is the most self-sufficient. It provides man almost effort-lessly with food and clothing as well as shelter. The tents of the first shepherds were made of animal skins. Of such was the roof on the ark; and of none other was the tabernacle of Moses. Concerning agriculture, which is slower to come into being: it is connected to all the arts; it leads to property, government, and laws, and gradually to the misery and crime that are inseparable for our species from the knowledge of good and evil. Nor did the Greeks consider Triptolemus merely as the inventor of a useful art, but as a teacher and sage from whom they received their initial formation and their first laws. On the other hand, Moses seems to have frowned upon agriculture in ascribing its invention to a reprobate, and having God reject its fruits. It is said that the first

---

[3] The craft of hunting is not at all favorable to population growth. This was observed when the islands of Santo Domingo and Tortuga were inhabited by buccaneers, and is confirmed by the condition of North America. No known founders of populous nations have been professional hunters. They have all been farmers or shepherds. Thus hunting must be treated here less as a means of subsistence than as an accessory of the pastoral condition.

farmer° proclaimed, in his character, the bad effects of
his art. The author of Genesis saw further than Herodotus.

To the preceding division there correspond the three
conditions of man considered in relation to society. The
savage is a hunter, the barbarian is a herdsman, and civil
man is a tiller of the soil.

When one investigates the origin of the arts and considers primitive customs, one sees that everything corresponds in its origin to the means of providing subsistence. And, as for those of these means that tend to
bring men together, they are determined by the climate
and by the nature of the soil. It is then by these same
causes that the diversity of tongues and their contrasting
characteristics must be explained.

The gentle climates, the fat and fertile lands, have
been the first to be inhabited and the last in which nations formed, because in them men could be satisfied
more easily than elsewhere and because there the needs
which give rise to social structures make themselves felt
later.

Supposing eternal spring on the earth; supposing
plenty of water, livestock, and pasture, and supposing
that men, as they leave the hands of nature, were once
spread out in the midst of all that, I cannot imagine
how they would ever be induced to give up their primitive liberty, abandoning the isolated pastoral life so
fitted to their natural indolence,⁴ to impose upon them-

° That is, Cain. Abel was a herdsman.—Tr.
⁴ It is not possible to determine the precise degree of man's natural
indolence. It is said that he lives only to sleep, to vegetate, to rest.
Only with difficulty can he resolve to bestir himself enough to
avoid dying of starvation. Nothing sustains the love of so many
savages for their mode of life as does this delicious indolence. The
feelings that make man restless, foresighted, and active arise only
in society. To do nothing is the primary and the strongest passion

selves unnecessarily the labors and the inevitable misery of a social mode of life.

He who willed man to be social, by the touch of a finger shifted the globe's axis into line with the axis of the universe. I see such a slight movement changing the face of the earth and deciding the vocation of mankind: in the distance I hear the joyous cries of a naive multitude; I see the building of castles and cities; I see the birth of the arts; I see nations forming, expanding, and dissolving, following each other like ocean waves; I see men leaving their homes, gathering to devour each other, and turning the rest of the world into a hideous desert: fitting monument to social union and the usefulness of the arts.

The earth nourishes men; but when their initial needs have dispersed them, other needs arise which reunite them, and it is only then that they speak, and that they have any incentive to speak. In order to avoid contradicting myself, I must be allowed time to explain myself.

If one lists the birthplaces of the founders of mankind, whence came the first settlements and the first emigrations, one does not name the happy climes of Asia Minor, Sicily, Africa, nor even Egypt, but the sands of Chaldea, the rocks of Phoenicia. You will find the same thing in any period. China has been populated by Chinese and it has also been populated by Tartars; the Scythians have flooded Europe and Asia; the mountains of Switzerland actually pour into our fertile regions a perpetual colony that shows no signs of ceasing.

It is said to be natural for the inhabitants of a barren land to leave it for a better one. Very well. But why do just these people swarm to just this better land, instead

---

of man after that of self-preservation. If one looks carefully, he will see that, just as among ourselves, it is in order to achieve repose that everyone works. It is laziness that even makes us hard-working.

of some other? It must be in order to leave a hostile country; yet why are so many born there out of preference? It is believed that barren countries are peopled only with the surplus population of fertile lands, and we see that the opposite is true. The majority of Latin peoples are considered aborigenes,[5] whereas Great Greece, much more fertile, was peopled only by foreigners. The people of Greece all derived from various colonies, except those whose soil was the worst, namely the Attic people, who call themselves autochthonous, or self-born. Finally, without piercing the night of time, modern centuries afford a crucial observation. For what climate on earth is more wretched than that of what is called "the workshop of the world"?

Human associations are due largely to accidents of nature: particular floods, extravasations of the seas, volcanic eruptions, earthquakes, fires started by lightning and destroying forests, all were bound to frighten and disperse the savage inhabitants of a country, and were bound to bring them together afterward, for a common effort to recoup their common losses. Traditions of earthly calamities, so frequent in ancient times, show what instruments Providence uses to reunite people. Since societies have been established, these great accidents have ceased, or have become less frequent. It seems that is bound to be true even now. The same evils that unite separated people tend to separate those who are united.

The cycles of the seasons are another more general and more permanent cause that is bound to produce the same effect in the climates subject to this variety. Forced to provide for winter, people living under such conditions

---

[5] The names *autochthon* and *aborigine* signify only that the earliest inhabitants of the country were savages, without laws, without traditions, and that the countries were populated before the development of speech.

have to establish some sort of convention among themselves in order to help each other.

When the rigors of frigid weather make it impossible to get about, boredom tends to unite them as much as need: the Lapps, buried in ice; and the Eskimos, the most savage of people, huddle all winter in their caverns, and then in summer do not even know each other any more. Given somewhat greater development and enlightenment, and there you have, *mutatis mutandis*, any social union.

Neither the stomach nor the intestines of man are made to digest raw meat, nor does it usually suit his taste. With the possible single exception of the Eskimos, of whom I am going to speak, even savages cook their meat.

To the necessary use of fire for cooking is joined the pleasure it gives to the eye and the warmth so comforting to the body. The sight of the flames, from which animals flee, is attractive to man.[6] People gather around a common hearth where they feast and dance; the gentle bonds of habit tend imperceptibly to draw man closer to his own kind. And on this simple hearth burns the sacred fire that provokes in the depths of the heart the first feeling of humanity.

In warm countries, unevenly distributed springs and rivers are even more necessary rallying agents than other such factors, since people are less able to do without water than fire. The barbarians especially, living off their

---

[6] Fire gives animals great pleasure, just as it does man, once they have become used to the sight of it, and felt its gentle warmth. Often it will prove almost as useful to them as to us, at least for warming their young. Still, no one would say that any beast, wild or domestic, has acquired the skill to make a fire in the same way that we do. Thus these rational beings who are said to have formed a short-lived society before man, still did not reach a level of intelligence at which they were able to strike a few sparks from a flint to make a fire, or even to preserve whatever random fires they might come across.

herds, need common watering places. And we learn from
the history of the earliest times that, in effect, this is
where both their treaties and their disputes originated.[7]
The flowing of waters can retard the society of people
inhabiting well-irrigated places. On the other hand, in
arid areas, there must be agreement on the sinking of
wells and the building of canals for watering livestock.
From time immemorial, men have united in such efforts,
for such a country must either remain desert or be made
habitable through human toil. But the penchant we have
for turning everything to our own use necessitates some
reflection on this point.

The original condition of the earth was quite different
from what it is today, when we see it as embellished or
marred by the hand of men. The chaos that poets at-
tribute to the elements actually reigns in their own pro-
ductions. In those remote times, when revolutions were
frequent, when a thousand accidents changed the nature
of the soil and the face of the earth, everything grew
confusedly. Trees, vegetables, shrubs, pasture: no species
had had time to appropriate land better suited to itself,
on which it could suppress others. They would separate
slowly, little by little, until suddenly a revolution would
occur, which would confuse everything.

There is a similar relation between human needs and
the products of the earth, which suffice for it to be peopled and for everyone to live. But before men could
reunite and achieve some order in their production,
through concerted effort, they had to live entirely according to nature, with no more stability than the hand of
men maintains today. Nature maintained or redressed
this balance by revolutions, while men maintained or
reestablished it through their inconstancy. War, which

---

[7] See Genesis XXI, for an example of each, between Abraham and
Abimilech, concerning the Well of Oath.

no longer reigned among them, seemed to reign among
the elements. Men did not burn cities, nor dig mines nor
fell trees at all. But nature ignited volcanoes and caused
earthquakes, lightning burned forests. A stroke of lightning, a flood, an eruption, could thus do in a few hours
what, under present conditions, takes fifty thousand men
a century. Otherwise I do not see how the system could
be kept standing and equilibrium be maintained. In the
two types of order, the greater species will finally absorb
the lesser.[8] The entire earth would soon be covered with
nothing but trees and ferocious beasts, and finally all
would perish.

The water cycle which vivifies the earth has gradually
lessened. The mountains are wearing down. The rivers
rush on, the sea fills up and expands, and everything
tends imperceptibly to level off. The hand of man curbs
this tendency and slows its progress; otherwise it would
be more rapid, perhaps the earth would already be under
water. Prior to human intervention, poorly distributed
springs flowed irregularly, so that the earth was less
effectively enriched and it was more difficult for its inhabitants to get drinking water. Rivers would have been
inaccessible, their banks either steep or marshy. Human
art would not keep them within their banks, which they

---

[8] It is held that, by a sort of natural action and reaction, various
dominant species of animals would perpetually counterbalance each
other, which would take the place of equilibrium for them. It is
said that when the devouring species became overnumerous at the
expense of the devoured, the former would encounter a food short-
age which would force them to retrench and allow the others time
to replenish their ranks to a point at which they could again provide the others with abundant food, and at which they would start
again to diminish, while their devourers would repopulate once
again. But such an oscillation does not seem at all likely to me, for
in this arrangement there has to be a period in which the species
that is preyed upon builds up while the one that feeds on them
diminishes, and that seems to me against all reason.

would frequently overflow to the left or right, changing their direction and their course, diverging into various branches. Sometimes they would dry up, and sometimes quicksand would block the way to them, so that they might as well not have existed, for one would die of thirst in the midst of their waters.

How many arid countries are habitable only because of trenches and canals that men had drawn off from rivers! Almost all of Persia is able to live only by this artifice. Their canals help the Chinese to constitute a single people. Without theirs, the Netherlands would be inundated by rivers, as they would be by the sea without their dikes. Egypt, the most fertile land on earth, is habitable only because of human toil. In the great plains, where there are no rivers and the land is flat, wells are the only source. If then, the first people of whom mention is made in history did not live in lush countries or on flowing shores, it is not that these delightful climes were deserts, but rather that their numerous inhabitants, desirous of avoiding each other, would remain isolated for a longer time within their families, without communication. But in the arid places where water could be had only from wells, people had to rejoin one another to sink the wells, or at least to agree upon their use. Such must have been the origin of societies and languages in warm countries.

That is where the first ties were formed among families; there were the first rendezvous of the two sexes. Girls would come to seek water for the household, young men would come to water their herds. There eyes, accustomed to the same sights since infancy, began to see with increased pleasure. The heart is moved by these novel objects; an unknown attraction renders it less savage; it feels pleasure at not being alone. Imperceptibly, water becomes more necessary. The livestock become thirsty more often. One would arrive in haste and leave with regret. In that happy age when nothing marked the hours, nothing would oblige one to count them; the only measure of time would be the alternation of amusement and boredom. Under old oaks, conquerors of the years, an ardent youth will gradually lose his ferocity. Little by little they become less shy with each other. In trying to make oneself understood, one learns to explain oneself. There too, the original festivals developed. Feet skipped with joy, earnest gestures no longer sufficed, being accompanied by an impassioned voice; pleasure and desire mingled and were felt together. There at last was the true cradle of nations: from the pure crystal of the fountains flow the first fires of love.

What then! Before that time did men spring from the earth? Did generations succeed each other without any union of the sexes, and without anyone being understood? No: there were families, but there were no nations. There were domestic languages, but there were no popular ones. There were marriages but there was no love at all. Each family was self-sufficient and perpetuated itself exclusively by inbreeding. Children of the same parents grew up together and gradually they found ways of expressing themselves to each other: the sexes became obvious with age; natural inclination sufficed to unite them. Instinct held the place of passion; habit held the place of preference. They became husband and wife without ceasing to be brother and sister.[9] There would be nothing stimu-

---

[9] The first men would have had to marry their sisters. In the simplicity of primitive customs, this practice would easily perpetuate itself as long as families remained isolated, and even after the reunion of the most ancient peoples. But the law that prohibits it is no less sacred for its human ordination. Those who see it only in terms of the bond it forms among families, fail to see its most important aspect. Given the intimacy that domestic life is bound to establish between the two sexes, from the moment such a sacred law ceased to appeal to the heart and mind there would be no more

lating enough in that to loosen the tongue, nothing to provoke accents of ardent passion often enough to conventionalize them. And it was possible for men to say enough about their rare and minor needs to enable them to work together. One would start the basin of a fountain and the other would follow through and finish it, often without their coming to any kind of agreement, sometimes even without their seeing each other. In a word, in a mild climate with fertile land, it took all the animation of pleasurable feelings to start the people speaking. The first tongues, children of pleasure rather than need, long bore the mark of their father. They lost their seductive tone with the advent of feelings to which they had given birth, when new needs arose among men, forcing each to be mindful only of his own welfare, and to withdraw his heart into himself.

CHAPTER TEN

Formation of the Languages of the North

Eventually all men became similar, but the order of their progress is different. In southern climes, where nature is bountiful, needs are born of passion. In cold countries, where she is miserly, passions are born of need, and the languages, sad daughters of necessity, reflect their austere origin.

integrity among men and the most terrifying practices would soon bring about the destruction of mankind.

Although man becomes accustomed to extremes of wind, cold, sickness, and even hunger, he still has his breaking point. Falling prey to such cruel ordeals, the weak perish. The strong become stronger; there is no mean at all between vigor and death. That is why northern peoples are so robust. It is not, as it first seems, that the climate makes them so, but only those who are could stand it. And it is not surprising that children should have the strong constitution of their fathers.

One can see already that the men, being more robust, are bound to have less delicate voices. Their voices are bound to be rougher and stronger. Besides, what a difference between the touching inflections that express the stirrings of the soul, and the cries of physical needs! In those wretched climates where everything is dead for nine months of the year, where the sun warms the air for only a few weeks, to inform the inhabitants of the benefits they are missing, and prolong their misery; where the earth yields nothing except through toil, and where life seems to come more from the arms than the heart, where men are ceaselessly busy providing for their subsistence, they hardly think of pleasanter ties. Everything is limited by physical motives. Occasion dictates choice; facility dictates preference. The idleness that nurtures passion is replaced by work, which represses it. Instead of being concerned with living happily, one had to be concerned with living. Mutual need uniting men to a greater extent when sentiment has not done so, society would be formed only through industry. The ever-present danger of perishing would not permit of a language restricted to gesture. And, the first words among them were not *love me* [*aimez-moi*] but *help me* [*aidez-moi*].

These two expressions, although similar enough, are pronounced in a very different tone. The whole point was not to make someone feel something, but to make him understand. Thus what was needed was not vigor but clarity. For the accents which the heart does not provide, distinct articulation is substituted. And if some trace of nature remains in the form of the language, this too contributes to its austerity.

Northern men are not passionless, but their passions are, in effect, those of another species. The passions of the warm countries are voluptuous, relating to love and tenderness. Nature does so much for people there that they have almost nothing to do. Provided that an Asiatic has women and repose, he is contented. But in the north, where people consume a great deal, on barren soil, men are easily irritated, being subject to so many needs. Anything happening near them disturbs them. As they subsist only through effort, the poorer they are the more firmly they hold to the little they have. To approach them is to threaten their lives. This is what accounts for their irascible temper, their quickness to attack anyone who offends them. Thus too their most natural tone of voice is angry and menacing, and their words are always accompanied by emphatic articulation, which makes them harsh and loud.

CHAPTER ELEVEN

Reflections on These Differences

These, in my opinion are the most general physical causes of the characteristic differences of the primitive tongues. Those of the south are bound to be sonorous, accented, eloquent, and frequently obscure because of their power. Those of the north are bound to be dull, harsh, articulated, shrill, monotonous, and to have a clarity due more to vocabulary than to good construction. The modern tongues, with all their intermingling and recasting, still retain something of these differences. French, English, German: each is a language private to a group of men who help each other, or who become angry. But the ministers of the gods proclaiming sacred mysteries, sages giving laws to their people, leaders swaying the multitude, have to speak Arabic or Persian.[1] Our tongues are better suited to writing than speaking, and there is more pleasure in reading us than in listening to us. Oriental tongues, on the other hand, lose their life and warmth when they are written. The words do not convey half the meaning; all the effectiveness is in the tone of voice. Judging the Orientals from their books is like painting a man's portrait from his corpse.

For a proper appreciation of their actions, men must be considered in all their relationships: which we simply are not capable of doing. When we put ourselves in the position of others, we do not become what they must be, but remain ourselves, modified. And, when we think we are judging them rationally, we merely compare their prejudices to ours. Thus, if one who read a little Arabic and enjoyed leafing through the Koran were to hear Mohammed personally proclaim in that eloquent, rhythmic tongue, with that sonorous and persuasive voice, seducing first the ears, then the heart, every sentence alive with enthusiasm, he would prostrate himself, crying: Great prophet, messenger of God, lead us to glory, to martyrdom. We will conquer or die for you. Fanaticism always seems ridiculous to us, because there is no voice among

---

[1] Turkish is a northern tongue.

us to make it understood. Our own fanatics are not au-
thentic fanatics. They are merely rogues or fools. Instead
of inspirational inflections, our tongues allow only for
cries of diabolic possession.

CHAPTER TWELVE

The Origin of Music and Its Relations

With the first voices came the first articulations or sounds
formed according to the respective passions that dictated
them. Anger produces menacing cries articulated by the
tongue and the palate. But the voice of tenderness is
softer: its medium is the glottis. And such an utterance
becomes a sound. It may occur with ordinary or unusual
tones, it may be more or less sharply accented, according
to the feeling to which it is joined. Thus rhythm and
sounds are born with syllables: all voices speak under
the influence of passion, which adorns them with all their
éclat. Thus verse, singing, and speech have a common
origin. Around the fountains of which I spoke, the first
discourses were the first songs. The periodic recurrences
and measures of rhythm, the melodious modulations of
accent, gave birth to poetry and music along with language. Or, rather that was the only language in those
happy climes and happy times, when the only pressing
needs that required the agreement of others were those to
which the heart gave birth.

The first tales, the first speeches, the first laws, were in

verse. Poetry was devised before prose. That was bound
to be, since feelings speak before reason. And so it was
bound to be the same with music. At first, there was no
music but melody and no other melody than the varied
sounds of speech. Accents constituted singing, quantity
constituted measure, and one spoke as much by natural
sounds and rhythm as by articulations and words. To
speak and to sing were formerly one, says Strabo, which
shows that in his opinion poetry is the source of eloquence.[1] It should be said that both had the same source,
not that they were initially the same thing. Considering
the way in which the earliest societies were bound together, is it surprising that the first stories were in verse
and the first laws were sung? Is it surprising that the first
grammarians subordinated their art to music and were
professors of both?[2]

A tongue which has only articulations and words has
only half its riches. True, it expresses ideas; but for the
expression of feelings and images it still needs rhythm
and sounds, which is to say melody, something the Greek
tongue has and ours lacks.

We are always astonished by the prodigious effects of
eloquence, poetry, and music among the Greeks. These
effects are incomprehensible to our minds because we do
not try to do such things any more. All that we can manage is to appear to believe them out of kindness toward

---

[1] *Geography,* Bk. I.

[2] "*Archytas atque Aristoxenes etiam subjectam grammaticen musi-
cae putaverunt, et eosdem utriusque rei praeceptores fuisse. . . .
Tum Eupolis, apud quem Prodamus et musicen et litteras docet.
Et Maricas, qui est Hyperbolus, nihil se ex musicis scire nisi litteras
Confitetur.*" Quintillian, Bk. I, ch. 10.

["Archytas and Aristoxenes also considered grammar to be in-
cluded under music, and the same masters taught both. . . . Then
too, Eupolus has Prodamus teaching both music and letters. And
Maricas, who is Hyperbolus, admits that he knows nothing of
music except letters."]

our scholars.[3] Burette, having translated certain Greek
musical pieces as well as could be, into our musical nota-
tion, was simple enough to have them played at the Academy of Belles-Lettres; and the academicians were patient
enough to listen to them. Such an experiment is admirable, in a country whose music all other nations find
indescribable. Ask any foreign musician to perform a
French operatic monologue and I defy you to recognize
any part of it. Yet these are the same Frenchmen who
purport to determine the melody of an ode of Pindar set
to music two thousand years ago!

I have read that the Indians in America, having seen
the amazing results of firearms, would gather musket balls
from the ground; they would throw them by hand, making a loud noise with the mouth. They were quite surprised that they did not kill anyone. Our orators, our
musicians, and our scholars are like these Indians. It is
not remarkable that we do not do as much with our music
as the Greeks did with theirs. On the contrary, it would be
remarkable if one produced the same results with such
different instruments.

---

[3] No doubt allowance must be made for Greek exaggeration in all
such matters; but one concedes too much to modern prejudice if
one pushes such discounting to the point where all differences vanish. "When Greek music in the time of Amphion and Orpheus had
reached the level it has attained today in the remotest provincial
cities," says Abbé Terrasson, "it would interrupt the course of
rivers, attract oak trees, and move cliffs. Today, having reached a
very high degree of perfection, it is very much loved, it is just as
pervasively beautiful, but it leaves everything in place. Thus, for
example, it includes the verses of Homer, a poet born in the infancy of the human spirit, compared to those who followed. We are
enraptured by these verses, but today we are content simply to enjoy and esteem those good poets." Undoubtedly the Abbé Terrasson
has had some acquaintance with philosophy, but he does not show
it in this passage.

CHAPTER THIRTEEN

On Melody

No one doubts that man is changed by his feelings. But instead of distinguishing the changes, we confuse them with their causes. We attach far too little importance to sensations. We do not see that frequently they have no effect on us merely as sensations, but as signs or images, and also that their moral effects have moral causes. Just as the feelings that a painting excites in us are not at all due to colors, the power of music over our souls is not at all the work of sounds. Beautiful, subtly shaded colors are a pleasing sight; but this is purely a pleasure of the sense. It is the drawing, the representation, which gives life and spirit to these colors. The passions they express are what stir ours; the objects they represent are what affect us. Colors entail no interest or feeling at all. The strokes of a touching picture affect us even in a print. Without these strokes in the picture, the colors would do nothing more.

The role of melody in music is precisely that of drawing in a painting. This is what constitutes the strokes and figures, of which the harmony and the sounds are merely the colors. But, it is said, melody is merely a succession of sounds. No doubt. And drawing is only an arrangement of colors. An orator uses ink to write out his compositions: does that mean ink is a very eloquent liquid?

Imagine a country in which no one has any idea of drawing, but where many people who spend their lives combining and mixing various shades of color are considered to excel at painting. Those people would regard our painting precisely as we consider Greek music. If they heard of the emotions aroused in us by beautiful paintings, the spell of a pathetic scene, their scholars would rush into a ponderous investigation of the material, comparing their colors to ours, determining whether our green is more delicate or our red more brilliant. They would try to find out which color combinations drew tears, which could arouse anger. The Burettes of that country would examine just a few tattered scraps of our paintings. Then they would ask with surprise what is so remarkable about such coloring.

And, if a start were made in a neighboring country toward the development of line and stroke, an incipient drawing, some still imperfect figure, it would all be treated as merely capricious, baroque daubing. And, for the sake of taste, one would cling to this simple style, which really expresses nothing, but brilliantly produces beautiful nuances, big slabs of color, long series of gradually shaded hues, without a hint of drawing.

Finally, the power of progress would lead to experiments with the prism. And immediately some famous artist would base a beautiful system on it. Gentlemen, he will tell you, true philosophy requires that things be traced to physical causes. Behold the analysis of light; behold the primary colors; observe their relations, their proportions. These are the true principles of the pleasure that painting gives you. All this mysterious talk of drawing, representation, figure, is just the charlatanry of French painters who think that by their imitations they can produce I know not what stirrings of the spirit, while it is known that nothing is involved but sensation. You hear of the marvels of their pictures; but look at my colors.

French painters, he would continue, may have seen a rainbow. Nature may have given them some taste for nuance, some sense of color. But I have revealed to you the great and true principles of art. I say of art! of all the arts, gentlemen, and of all the sciences. The analysis of colors, the calculation of prismatic refractions, give you the only exact relations in nature, the rule of all relations. And everything in the universe is nothing but relations. Thus one knows everything when one knows how to paint; one knows everything when one knows how to match colors.

What are we to say of a painter sufficiently devoid of feeling and taste to think like that, stupidly restricting the pleasurable character of his art to its mere mechanics? What shall we say of a musician, similarly quite prejudiced, who considers harmony the sole source of the great effects of music. Let us consign the first to housepainting and condemn the other to doing French opera.

Music is no more the art of combining sounds to please the ear than painting is the art of combining colors to please the eye. If there were no more to it than that, they would both be natural sciences rather than fine arts. Imitation alone raises them to this level. But what makes painting an imitative art? Drawing. What makes music another? Melody.

CHAPTER FOURTEEN

On Harmony

The beauty of sounds is natural. Their effect is purely physical. It is due to the coincidence of various particles of air set in motion by the sonorous body and all their aliquots, perhaps to infinity: the total effect is pleasing. Everyone in the world takes pleasure in hearing beautiful sounds. But if the pleasure is not enlivened by melodious inflections that are familiar to them, it will not be at all delightful, will not become at all voluptuous. The songs most beautiful to us will only moderately move those to whom they are quite unfamiliar. It is a tongue for which one needs a dictionary.

Harmony, properly speaking, is a still more difficult matter. Being only conventionally beautiful, it does not in any way please the completely unpracticed ear. Development of sensitivity and taste for it requires long exposure. To the uncultured ear, our consonances are merely noise. It is not surprising that when natural proportions are impaired, the corresponding natural pleasure is destroyed.

A sound is accompanied by all its concomitant harmonic sounds so related in terms of power and interval as to harmonize most perfectly with that sound. Join to it the third or fifth or some other consonance; you do not join anything to it, you redouble it. You retain the relation of interval while changing that of force. By intensifying one consonance and not the others, you break up the proportion. In trying to do better than nature, you do worse. Your ear and your taste are impaired by a poor understanding of the art. Naturally, the only harmony is unison.

M. Rameau proposes that, by a certain unity, each treble naturally suggests its bass and that an untrained person with a true ear will naturally begin to sing that bass. That is the prejudice of a musician, against all experience. Not only will those who have no idea of either bass or harmony fail to find it, but even if they could be made to understand it, they would be displeased by it, preferring simple unison.

Even if one spent a thousand years calculating the relations of sounds and the laws of harmony, how would one ever make of that art an imitative art? Where is the principle of this supposed imitation? Of what harmony is it the sign? And what do chords have in common with our passions?

When the same question is applied to melody, the reply is the same: it is in the mind of the reader beforehand. By imitating the inflections of the voice, melody expresses pity, cries of sorrow and joy, threats and groans. All the vocal signs of passion are within its domain. It imitates the tones of languages, and the twists produced in every idiom by certain psychic acts [*mouvemens de l'âme*]. Not only does it imitate, it bespeaks. And its language, though inarticulate, is lively, ardent, passionate; and it has a hundred times the vigor of speech itself. This is what gives music its power of representation and song its power over sensitive hearts. In certain systems, harmony can bring about unification through binding the succession of sounds according to laws of modulation; rendering intonation more appropriate and offering some definite aural evidence of this aptness; fixing and reconciling consonant intervals, and coordinating imperceptible inflections. But in the process it also shackles melody, draining it of energy and expressiveness. It wipes out passionate accent, replacing it with the harmonic interval. It is restricted to only two types of songs, within which its possibilities are determined by the number of oral tones. It eliminates many sounds or intervals which do not fit into its system. Thus in brief, it separates singing from speech, setting these two languages against each other to their mutual deprivation of all authenticity, so that it is absurd for them to occur together in a pathetic subject. That is why the expression of strong and serious passion in song always seems ridiculous, for it is known that in our languages the passions have no musical inflection at all, and that northern peoples do not die singing any more than swans do.

By itself, harmony is insufficient even for those expressions that seem to depend uniquely on it. Thunder, murmuring waters, winds, tempests, are but poorly rendered by simple harmonies. Whatever one does, noise alone does not speak to the spirit at all. The objects of which one speaks must be understood. In all imitation, some form of discourse must substitute for the voice of nature. The musician who would represent noise by noise deceives himself. He knows nothing of either the weakness or the strength of his art, concerning which his judgment is tasteless and unenlightened.

Let him realize that he will have to render noise in song; that to produce the croaking of frogs, he will have to have them sing. For it is not enough to imitate them; he must do so touchingly and pleasantly. Otherwise, his tedious imitation is nothing, and will neither interest nor impress anyone.

CHAPTER FIFTEEN

That Our Most Lively Sensations Frequently Are Produced by Moral Impressions

As much as one might want to consider sounds only in terms of the shock that they excite in our nerves, this would not touch the true principle of music, nor its power over men's hearts. The sounds of a melody do not affect us merely as sounds, but as signs of our affections, of our feelings. It is thus that they excite in us the emotions which it expresses, whose image we recognize in it. Something of this moral effect is perceivable even in animals. The barking of one dog will attract another. When my cat hears me imitate a mewing, I see it become immediately attentive, alert, agitated. When it discovers that I am just counterfeiting the voice of its species, it relaxes and resumes its rest. Since there is nothing at all different in the stimulation of the sense organ, and the cat had initially been deceived, what accounts for the difference?

Unless the influence of sensations upon us is due mainly to moral causes, why are we so sensitive to impressions that mean nothing to the uncivilized? Why is our most touching music only a pointless noise to the ear of a West Indian? Are his nerves of a different nature from ours? Why are they not excited in the same way? Or, why should the same stimulus excite some people very much and others so little?

The healing of tarantula bites is cited in proof of the physical power of sounds. But in fact this evidence proves quite the opposite. What is needed for curing those bitten by this insect are neither isolated sounds, nor even simply tunes. Rather, each needs tunes with familiar melodies and understandable lyrics. Italian tunes are needed for Italians; for Turks, Turkish tunes. Each is affected only by accents familiar to him. His nerves yield only to what his spirit predisposes them. One must speak to him in a language he understands, if he is to be moved by what he is told. The cantatas of Bernier are said to have cured the fever of a French musician. They would have given one to a musician of any other nation.

The same differences can be observed relative to the other senses, even the crudest. Suppose a man has his hand placed and his eyes fixed upon the same object, while he alternately believes it to be alive and not alive: the effect on his senses would be the same, but what a different impression! Roundness, whiteness, firmness, pleasant warmth, springy resistance, and successive rising, would give him only a pleasant but insipid feeling if he did not believe he felt a heart full of life beating under it all.

I know of only one affective sense in which there is no moral element: that is taste. And, accordingly, gluttony is the main vice only of those who have no sense of taste.

If those who philosophize about the power of sensations would begin by distinguishing pure sense impressions from the intellectual and moral impressions received through the senses, but of which the senses are only the occasional causes, they would avoid the error of attributing to sense objects a power they do not have, or that they have only in relation to affections of the soul which they represent to us. Colors and sounds can do much, as representatives and signs, very little simply as objects of sense. Series of sounds or of chords will perhaps amuse me for a moment; but to charm me and soften me, these series must offer something that is neither sound nor chord, and moves me in spite of myself. Even songs that are merely pleasant but say nothing, are tiresome. For the ear does not so much convey pleasure to the heart as the heart conveys it to the ear. I believe that through developing these ideas, we shall be spared stupid arguments about ancient music. But in this century when all the operations of the soul have to be materialized, and deprived of all morality and human feeling, I am deluded if the new philosophy does not become as destructive of good taste as of virtue.

CHAPTER SIXTEEN

False Analogy between Colors and Sounds

There is no kind of absurdity that has not been given a place in the treatment of fine arts by physical observation. The same relations have been discovered in the analysis of sound as in the analysis of light. This analogy has been seized upon immediately and eagerly, with no concern for reason or experience. The systematizing spirit has confused everything, and presumes, out of ignorance, to paint for the ears and sing for the eyes. I have seen the famous clavichord on which music is supposedly made

with colors. It would be a complete misunderstanding of
the workings of nature not to see that the effect of colors
is in their stability and that that of sounds is in their succession.

All the riches of color display themselves at a given
moment. Everything is taken in at first glance. But the
more one looks, the more one is enchanted; one need only
admire and contemplate, endlessly.

This is not true of sound. Nature does not analyze
sounds or isolate harmonics. On the contrary, it hides
such distinctions under the appearance of unison. Or, if
it does sometimes separate them, as in the modulated
singing of man and the warbling of some birds, it is in
succession, one after the other. Nature inspires songs, not
accords; she speaks of melody, not harmony. Colors are
the clothing of inanimate objects. All matter is colored.
But sounds manifest movement. A voice bespeaks a sensitive being. Only living bodies sing. It is not an automatic
flute player that plays the flute; it is the engineer who
measured the wind and made the fingers move.

Thus each sense has its proper domain. The domain of
music is time; that of painting is space. To multiply the
sounds heard at a given time, or to present colors in
sequence, is to alter their economy, putting the eye in the
place of the ear, and the ear in the place of the eye.

You say: Just as color is determined by the angle of
refraction of the ray it emits, each sound is determined by
the number of vibrations of a sounding object in a given
time period. But the relations of these angles and of these
numbers will be the same. The analogy is evident. Agreed.
Yet this analogy is rational, not experiential. So this is not
an issue. The angle of refraction is primarily experiential and measurable, while the number of vibrations is
not. Sounding bodies, subject to air currents, incessantly
change in volume and tone. Colors are durable, sounds

vanish. And one is never sure that later sounds will be the same as those that preceded. Further, each color is absolute and independent while each sound is, for us, only relative, distinguished only by comparison. A sound, considered in itself, has no absolute character by which it is recognizable. It is hard or soft, has an acute or grave accent in relation to another. In itself, none of this applies to it. Even in the harmonic system, no sound is anything by nature. It is neither tonic, nor dominant, nor harmonic nor fundamental, because all these properties are only relational; and because the whole system could vary from grave to acute, each sound changing its rank and position in the system according to the extent to which the system itself changes. But the properties of colors are not at all relational. Yellow is yellow, independently of red and of blue. Everywhere it is sensate and recognizable. As soon as its angle of refraction is determined, one can be certain that one has the same yellow at all times.

The locus of colors is not in colored bodies, but in light. For an object to be visible, it must be illuminated. Sounds also need a mover, and in order for them to exist, a sonorous body must be struck. This is another advantage of sight, for the perpetual emanation of the stars is its natural stimulus, while nature alone engenders little sound. And, unless one believes in the harmony of the celestial spheres, it must be produced by living beings.

From this it is evident that painting is closer to nature and that music is more dependent on human art. It is evident also that the one is more interesting than the other precisely because it does more to relate man to man, and always gives us some idea of our kind. Painting is often dead and inanimate. It can carry you to the depths of the desert; but as soon as vocal signs strike your ear, they announce to you a being like yourself. They are, so to speak, the voice of the soul. If you hear them in the wilderness, they tell you you are not there alone. Birds whistle; man alone sings. And one cannot hear either singing or a symphony without immediately acknowledging the presence of another intelligent being.

It is one of the great advantages of the musician that he can represent things that cannot be heard, while it is impossible to represent in painting things which cannot be seen. And the greatest marvel, for an art whose only medium is motion, is to represent repose. Sleep, the calm of night, even silence, enter into musical pictures. It is known that noise can produce the effect of silence, and silence the effect of noise, as when one falls asleep at a dull monotonous lecture and wakes up as soon as it ends. But music affects us more deeply, arousing through one sense feelings similar to those aroused through another. But, since its result must be perceptible, and its impression weak, painting lacks this power: it cannot imitate music as music can imitate it. Even if the whole of nature were asleep, those who contemplate it would not be. And the musician's art consists of substituting for an imperceptible image of the object the movements which its presence excites in the heart of the contemplator. Not only will it agitate the sea, fan flames, and engorge a stream, but it will depict the horrors of a frightening wilderness, darken the walls of a dungeon, calm a tempest, subdue the winds, and the orchestra will lavish new freshness upon the forest. It does not represent these things directly, but excites in the soul the same feelings one experiences in seeing them.

CHAPTER SEVENTEEN

An Error of Musicians
Harmful to Their Art

See how everything continually takes us back to the moral effects of which I spoke, and how far from understanding the power of their art are those many musicians who think of the potency of sounds only in terms of air pressure and string vibrations. The more they assimilate it to purely physical impressions, the farther they get from its source and the more they deprive it of its primitive energy. In dropping its oral tone and sticking exclusively to the establishment of harmonics, music becomes noisier to the ear and less pleasing to the heart. As soon as it stops singing, it stops speaking. And then, with all its accord and all its harmony it will have no more effect upon us.

CHAPTER EIGHTEEN

That the Greek Musical System Had No Relation to Ours

How have such changes occurred? Through a natural change in the character of the tongues. It is known that our harmony is a Gothic invention. Those who claim to find the system of the Greeks in ours are ridiculous. The Greek system was absolutely devoid of harmonics in our sense, which requires the instruments to be tuned to perfect agreement. Stringed instruments always have to be tuned in consonance. But people who do not use stringed instruments have inflections in their singing which we consider false because they do not fit into our system and we do not care to note them. This can be observed in the singing of American savages, and is bound to be observable in various periods of Greek music too, if it is studied without a prejudice in favor of our own. The Greeks divided their scale by tetrachords, as we divide our keyboard by octaves; and the same divisions were repeated in each of their tetrachords as are repeated in each of our octaves. This is a similitude which could not be preserved and would not even be suspected, in the unity of harmonic mode. But since one proceeds by smaller intervals in speaking than in singing, it would be natural for them to treat the repetition of tetrachords in their oral melody as we treat the repetition of octaves in our harmonic melody.

The only consonances they would recognize are those we call perfect consonances. They would preclude thirds and sixths from this category. Why was that? Because they ignored, or at least in practice they proscribed, the minor tone interval. And their consonances were not at all tempered. All their major thirds were too strong and their minor thirds too weak for a comma. Consequently their major and minor sixths were reciprocally impaired in the same way. Just think what our idea of harmony would be, and what harmonic modes could be established by eliminating thirds and sixths as consonances. If they had any real sense of harmony, even for those consonances they did allow, their songs would have contained, at least implicitly, the consonance of fundamental progressions which, having given its name to the diatonic scale, would have suggested it to them. Rather than having fewer consonances than we, they would have had more. And, preoccupied by the bass *ut sol* for example, they would have called the second *ut re,* a consonance.

But then why speak of diatonic progressions? In accord with our inclination to choose the most convenient inflections in an accented and singable language. Because of the extremely difficult glottal stops involved in the long intervals of the consonances, and the difficulty of controlling intonation in the very complicated relations of shorter intervals, the voice takes a middle course, falling naturally upon intervals shorter than consonances and simpler than commas. And yet the shorter intervals did not have the same use as they, in the more affective genres.

CHAPTER NINETEEN

How Music Has Degenerated

To the degree that language improved, melody, being
governed by new rules, imperceptibly lost its former
energy, and the calculus of intervals was substituted for
nicety of inflection. That is how, for example, the sub-
harmonic genre gradually fell into disuse. When the theaters had taken a regular form, all singing was according to prescribed modes. And, to the degree that the rules
of limitation proliferated, imitative language was en-
feebled.

The study of philosophy and the progress of reason,
while having perfected grammar, deprive language of its
vital, passionate quality which made it so singable. Com-
posers, who originally were engaged by poets and worked
only for them, under their direction so to speak, were becoming independent as early as the time of Melanippides
and Philoxenus. This is the license of which Music com-
plains so bitterly in a comedy of Pherecrates, according
to the passage preserved by Plutarch. Thus melody,
originally an aspect of discourse, imperceptibly assumes
a separate existence and music becomes more independent of speech. That is also when it stopped producing the
marvels it had produced when it was merely the accent
and harmony of poetry and gave to it the power over the
passions that speech subsequently exercised only on rea-

son. Also, Greece was then full of sophists and philosophers, though she no longer had any famous musicians or poets. In cultivating the art of convincing, that of arousing the emotions was lost. Plato himself, envious of Homer and Euripides, decried the one and was unable to imitate the other.

Servitude soon joined forces with philosophy. In fetters, Greece lost the fire that warms only free spirits, and in praising her tyrants, she never recovered the style in which she had sung her heroes. The intermingling of the Romans further weakened whatever harmony and accent remained to the language. Latin, a less musical, more surded tongue, did harm to the music in adopting it. The singing employed in the capital gradually corrupted that of the provinces. The Roman theaters were sustained by those of Athens. When Nero carried off the prize, Greece had ceased to merit it. And the same melodiousness, parceled between two tongues, is less well suited to either.

Finally came the catastrophe that disrupted the progress of the human spirit without removing the faults that were its product. Europe, flooded with barbarians, enslaved by ignoramuses, lost at the same time her sciences, her arts, and that universal instrument of both: that is, harmoniously perfected language. Imperceptibly, every ear became accustomed to the rude voices of these coarse men engendered by the North. Their harsh, expressionless voices were noisy without being sonorous. The Emperor Julian compared Gallic speech to the croaking of frogs. All their articulations, like their voices, being nasal and muffled, they could give only some kind of distinctness to their singing, augmenting the vowel sounds to cover up the abundance and harshness of the consonants.

The noisy singing, along with the monotonous voices, forced the newcomers and their subjects, who imitated them, to say everything slowly in order to be understood. The laborious enunciation and the exaggerated sounds contributed equally to the elimination of all sense of measure and rhythm from melody. Since most of their difficulty of pronunciation would be in making transitions from one sound to another, there was nothing better to do than hesitate at each as long as possible to expand it, making it as distinct as possible. Singing soon became no more than a slow, tiresome sequence of drawling sounds and yells, without softness, without measure, and without grace. Should any scholars point out that it was necessary to observe the long and the short syllables in Latin singing, it is certain at least that verses were sung as prose, with no further question of feet or rhythm nor any other kind of measured singing.

That singing was thus devoid of melody, consisting solely of volume and duration of the sounds, was bound to suggest at last a way of making it more melodious again, with the help of the consonances. Several voices, ceaselessly drawling sounds of unlimited duration, in unison, happened upon some harmonies, which seemed pleasant to them because they added to the noise. And thus began the practice of descant and of counterpoint.

I skip many centuries during which the musicians pondered vain questions, the result, as is known, of ignoring a principle. Even the most indefatigable reader will not wade through eight or ten long chapters of Jean de Muris' verbiage to learn whether it is the fifth or the fourth that is to be flat in the interval of an octave divided into two consonances. And four hundred years later, in Bontempi, one finds equally tedious enumerations of all the basses that must carry the sixth instead of the fifth. Thus harmony imperceptibly took the course prescribed for it by analysis, until finally the invention of the minor mode and of dissonances introduced the arbitrariness of which it is full, and which only prejudice prevents our perceiving.[1]

Melody was forgotten when musicians gave their full attention to harmony, gradually letting themselves be governed entirely according to this novelty. The genres, the modes, the scale, all received new faces. Harmonic successions came to dictate the sequence of parts. This sequence having usurped the name of melody, it was, in effect, impossible to recognize the traits of its mother in this new melody. And our musical system having thus gradually become purely harmonic, it is not surprising that its oral tone had suffered, and that our music had lost almost all its energy.

Thus we see how singing gradually became an art entirely separate from speech, from which it takes its origin; how the harmonics of sounds resulted in forgetting vocal inflections; and finally, how music, restricted to

---

[1] Relating all harmony to the very simple principle of the reverberation of notes in their aliquots, M. Rameau bases the minor mode and dissonance on his supposed observation that the motion of a sonorous string produces vibrations in other strings, longer than its twelfth and its seventeenth flat major. According to him, the strings vibrate and quiver over their entire length, but do not reverberate. This strikes me as physically unique, as if one said the sun shone but nothing was seen.

The longer strings produce only sharps, because they divide, vibrate, resound in unison, and blend that sound with their own, apparently making no sound. The error is in thinking they vibrate over their entire length, failing to observe the knots carefully. Two sonorous strings forming some harmonic interval can make their fundamental and flat sound heard even without a third string. This is a matter of experience, confirmed by M. Tartini. But a single string has no other fundamental note than its own. It produces no resonance or vibration in its multiples, but only in its unison and its aliquots. As sound has no other cause than the vibration of bodies, and where the cause acts freely the effect always follows, it is absurd to speak of separating vibrations from resonance.

purely physical concurrences of vibrations, found itself
deprived of the moral power it had yielded when it was
the twofold voice of nature.

CHAPTER TWENTY

Relationship of Languages to Government

These developments are neither fortuitous nor arbitrary.
They belong to the vicissitudes of things. The languages
develop naturally on the basis of men's needs, changing
and varying as those needs change. In ancient times,
when persuasion played the role of public force, eloquence was necessary. Of what use would it be today,
when public force has replaced persuasion. One needs
neither art nor metaphor to say *such is my pleasure*.
What sort of public discourses remain then? Sermons.
And why should those who preach them be concerned
to persuade the people, since it is not they who dispose
of benefices. Our popular tongues have become just as
completely useless as eloquence. Societies have assumed
their final form: no longer is anything changed except by
arms and cash. And since there is nothing to say to people
besides *give money*, it is said with placards on street
corners or by soldiers in their homes. It is not necessary
to assemble anyone for that. On the contrary, the subjects must be kept apart. That is the first maxim of modern politics.

There are some tongues favorable to liberty. They

are the sonorous, prosodic, harmonious tongues in which discourse can be understood from a great distance. Ours are made for murmuring on couches. Our preachers torment themselves, work themselves into a sweat in the pulpit without anyone knowing anything of what they have said. After exhausting themselves shouting for an hour, they collapse in a chair, half dead. Surely it would not be work that fatigues them so.

It was easy for the ancients to make themselves understood by people in public. They could speak all day with no discomfort. Generals could address their troops and be understood, with no exhaustion at all. Modern historians who wanted to include harangues in their account would be able to do no more than caricature them. If a man were to harangue the people of Paris in the Place Vendôme in French, if he shouted at the top of his voice, people would hear him shouting, but they would not be able to distinguish a word. Herodotus would recite his history to Greek audiences in the open air, and everyone would restrain himself from applauding. Today, the people in the rear of the room strain to hear an academician read a memorandum at a public assembly. If charlatans are less common in the public squares of France than in those of Italy, it is not because they would receive less attention in France, but only because they would not be as well understood. M. d'Alembert thought that French recitative could be sold to the Italians. Then it would have to be sold to the ear, or it would not be understood at all. But I say that any tongue with which one cannot make oneself understood to the people assembled is a slavish tongue. It is impossible for a people to remain free and speak that tongue.

These superficial reflections, which hopefully might give birth to more profound ones, I shall conclude with the passage that suggested them to me:

To observe in fact and to show by examples, the degree to which the character, customs and interests of a people influence their language, would provide material for a sufficiently philosophical investigation.[1]

---

[1] M. Duclos, *Remarques sur la grammaire générale et raisonnée,* p. 2.

AFTERWORD

For Rousseau, the "origin of languages" is a peculiarly enigmatic but crucial element in his speculative account of how things came to be as they are: the transition from a state of nature through institutional forms to civil society. This etiology of the human condition, a secular version of the Fall, is the dominant theme of his work. With respect to language, he is mainly concerned with distinguishing and clarifying the conditions that motivate men to speak: the differences that language makes in men's lives, and changes in the basic character of language wrought by changes in our ways of living.

Rousseau's is a prominent voice, that of a soloist standing out from the chorus of the great refusal, the great rejection of demands externally imposed upon individuals in the formal, conventional, artificial, political, frequently arbitrary environment of civil society. But he does not simply reject civil society, of whose benefits as well as impositions he is a keen and eloquent analyst. He objected less to life according to law, than to life under law posited and applied by the will of another; an alien will.

His critique of the "moral" world, the world designed and fabricated by men, is expressed positively as a paean to nature, which he tends to contrast with art. For him, nature is a primitive, interior, dynamic principle, at once proper to each individual and to the physical world as a whole. Art, manifesting itself in the political, military, pedagogical and industrial domains, as well as in "fine" arts, is the peculiarly human agency of actively dominating, exploiting, and transforming what is "natural" both in men and in things.

That these very expressions of human activity, by which men contrive intelligently to satisfy their needs, might be a basic source of human misery and corruption— the sweeping tragedy that men might be the prisoners of their own products and thus of their freedom—was a sad possibility that Rousseau confronted, explored, analyzed, and eloquently communicated.

Assessment of the human condition in terms of "opposite" categories such as nature and art, seems destined to issue in paradox. If "nature" is the inner source of all activity, then art is derivative of nature and to that degree "natural." This suggests, at least, an original division of nature against itself. What then of primitively pure nature corrupted by alien art?

We may merely hint at a reply. First, for Rousseau, as for a hoary tradition to which he belongs, an individual is not merely a replaceable unit, an instance of an abstract universal essence. Rather, each individual is unique, possessed of, even in some ways identical with, his own nature or "essence" while participating in the whole of nature, the whole of reality, so to speak. In so far as there is a plurality of individuals, and one individual (or group) practices any of the arts on others, there is a basis for contrasting nature (the nature of one) and art (the art of another).

Second, if one envisions nature as the inner dynamic of the whole of reality, while granting on empiric grounds that there is conflict, one will probably incline toward one of the following: (1) Empirically given conflicts constitute a division of nature against itself (2) Empiric conflicts belong to a realm of *mere* appearance; nature is (must be) one, though its unity does not appear, and (3) Nature, originally one, has suffered a rupture (or ruptures) that may be healed in a future renewal of unity, though the renewal would not be a simple repetition.

Of these three, the last most nearly fits Rousseau. Unwilling or unable to make a traditional resignation of his individuality to the immediate (political) universal, he turned his art to the achievement of a reunified nature, according to his own vision. This brought his art into conflict with that of others, most significantly though not exclusively with the practitioners of statecraft.

Undoubtedly cosmopolitan in spirit, Rousseau at his best objected to particular, fragmentary "universals" in the name of a universal universal, that is, nature. Yet his conceptions of social order apply only to a society that would be one among others. The notion of nature thus functions for Rousseau as a critical foil against authoritarianism and all forms of externalism, and as the key concept in his advocacy of interiority or liberty, which he conceived as strict obedience to self-imposed law.

In the "state of nature," men made only immediate responses to immediate situations, according to physical impulse, but in civil society their lives attain a new kind of stability as they live in terms of general categories, according to right and duty, justice and law, which transcend the immediate in both space and time. But concomitantly, there arises the possibility of wrongs, injustice, illegality, all of which are similarly transcendent. Beyond natural, physical liberty, the conditions are now present for moral liberty, the highest stage of which would amount to spontaneous universal cooperation, each individual obedient to all, but none subject to any particular and therefore private will or authority.

Not least significant in this view is the notion it entails

that "human nature" changes or at least develops according to changing needs and conditions of human life. Thus to the degree that men can know and control these conditions, they should be able to direct the process of human nature toward optimum conditions of liberty, in which art has become a second nature: not an original state of being, but a condition such as will allow the human potential to be fully realized.

Neither in style nor in fact was Rousseau detached from the problems he treated. It is not difficult to relate even the most abstract and general of his works to personal involvement. While the circumstances of his life may have determined the direction of his interests and the intensity of his preoccupation, they neither account for his genius nor vitiate his insights. His mother died several days after his birth in Geneva in 1712. During his childhood, he and his father, a watchmaker, often read novels together; sometimes, fascinated by the romantic tales, they stayed awake all night. At the age of seven, he began to read more serious works from the library of his maternal grandfather, a minister of religion.

When his father went into exile rather than go to prison for fighting with a French captain, the young Rousseau was left in the custody of his uncle. The latter sent him and his cousin to board with a young pastor, who served as their tutor for two years, after which they lived in the uncle's house for several years. Then, after a brief, boring stint in the city registrar's office, Rousseau was apprenticed to an engraver, who frequently beat him. There came an evening when Rousseau returned to the city after the gates were closed for the night, whereupon he decided to leave Geneva.

He found his way to Annecy where he met Mme. Warens, a Catholic convert under whose influence he became a Catholic. She sent him to Turin where he

worked as a valet and received instruction in Catholicism.
Returning to Annecy, he spent five months in a seminary,
then lived for about six years with Mme. Warens who
afforded him leisure for study and, though he regarded
her as a mother, she eventually became his mistress.

At thirty, he presented a new system of musical nota-
tion to the Academy of Science in Paris. There followed
a year as secretary to the French ambassador in Venice,
after which he returned to Paris where he agreed to
write articles on music for the *Encyclopedia* projected
by Diderot and D'Alembert. At that time he met Thérèse
Le Vasseur who became his mistress and the mother of
his five children, each of whom was abandoned at a
foundling home.

In 1750, Rousseau's *Discourse on the Sciences and the
Arts* won the essay competition of the Dijon Academy
on the question whether the restoration of sciences and
arts (the Renaissance) had been advantageous to morality. Arguing forcefully to the contrary, Rousseau now
began a voluminous literary output, developing variations
on his major theme: the relationships of nature and freedom.

In 1753, his short, highly mannered, pastoral opera,
Le Devin du Village (*The Village Soothsayer*), a fa-
vorite of the King, was first performed at the Paris Opera
House.

In his *Discourse on Inequality* of 1755 he sought the
origin of social artificialities which, he considered, derived from the institution of private property and from
human efforts to cope with growing necessities. It was
his view that the progress of human "perfectibility,"
through the development of skills and other abilities, exaggerated men's natural differences, and that by trying
to satisfy our needs we increase them.

The enormously popular *La Nouvelle Héloïse*, a novel

in which Rousseau depicted his ideal lovers and developed a morality of sentiment, appeared in 1761. The following year, two incalculably influential works, *The Social Contract* and *Émile*, were published. In the first, Rousseau sought to determine how a social order, inevitable in any case, might be constituted on a legitimate rational basis of popular sovereignty. The latter, a dissertation on natural education in the form of a novel, contains the fullest expression of Rousseau's thoughts on natural religion, the "Creed of a Priest of Savoy."

But Rousseau enjoyed little triumph. After a quarrel with his benefactress, Mme. d'Epinay, he departed from his beloved country retreat, L'Ermitage. *Émile* was condemned in Parliament, and in Paris it was burned. Further, having resumed his Genevan citizenship and membership of the Church of Geneva, he was to suffer the confiscation and burning of *Émile* and of *The Social Contract*, and the threat of arrest in that city. Indeed his life was now to be unsettled to the end, which came in 1778 at Ermenonville where he was the guest of the Marquis de Girardin.

The sections on music in the *Essay on the Origin of Languages* were written in 1749, apparently for the *Encyclopedia*. The remainder apparently belongs to the period of the *Discourse on the Origin of Inequality*. It seems Rousseau kept the *Essay* from publication in order to avoid further conflict with authority.

While accepting the view of the Encyclopedists that human institutions, including languages, arise to meet human needs, Rousseau opposed their restriction of such needs to immediate physical necessities. On the contrary, the latter, instead of drawing men into association, tend to disperse them. While their natural, physical needs tend to scatter men over the globe, what unites them into specific peoples, sharing common forms of life, are needs of a different and superior kind—moral needs, the need of people to relate to each other, which Rousseau sees as somehow independent of their need for food, shelter, clothing, and sexual gratification.

Since speech and writing are crucially social, their origins will be those of society; rather than deriving from the efforts of reason to satisfy physical necessity, they occur, in hospitable climates at least, primarily as musical and poetical expressions of emotion. The device of origin and development, the emphasis on the role of gesture and on signs other than verbal ones, help to make Rousseau's account of language more human than any treatment along static, essential lines. In our own day, its family resemblances to Ludwig Wittgenstein's *Philosophical Investigations* are sometimes striking. On the other hand, it also bears an unmistakable kinship to Wittgenstein's earlier work, the *Tractatus Logico-Philosophicus,* and to Bertrand Russell's "logical atomism," for Rousseau seems uncritically to share the common assumption that language can be meaningful only by being referential. In this respect, he is concerned only with broadening the essential scope of referents, beyond the physical and conceptual, to include the moral and passional. However, he does not attempt anything approaching Wittgenstein's or Russell's elaborate, *ex professo* systematic treatment of the referential relations, supposedly crucial to any meaningful use of language.

Since men unite socially even when they are under pressure to diverge, war is not natural to them: their interest in each other's attitudes, feelings, and wills is manifest in communion as well as competition. Far from being a necessary means to peace, as Hobbes argued, human society is the necessary precondition to war.

Although he emphasized moral and passional factors at the source of language, Rousseau himself is unable to understand sympathetically how men would take upon themselves the yoke of social forms unless pressed by direst necessity. It seems to be Rousseau's view that, since physical needs can both unite and disperse people under different circumstances, the two positions might be complementary. If not, he would be left with the paradox that confronted him in the *Discourse on Inequality:* society presupposes language and language presupposes society. Further, the most primitive beginnings of language imaginable would, in Rousseau's view, consist of a few gestures and inarticulate sounds, such as grunts and cries, proper to family groups. But genuine languages, the scope of whose use would be at least interfamilial, would presuppose or form part of, a wider social bond.

In general, the development of language corresponds for Rousseau to successive stages of social organization: savage, barbaric, civilized. The transition is from immediacy and spontaneity to generality and convention. The highest stage belongs to civilization, where increasingly the conventional utterances of our languages replace even the spontaneous cries of joy and pain proper to the childhood of both race and individual.

The three levels of social order are based upon three modes of getting a livelihood. The savage, who lives by hunting and fishing, needs only rudimentary implements which he can produce for himself. Barbarians live the pastoral life of herdsmen, which is virtually self-sufficient. Agriculture, in which civilization has its beginnings, presupposes a stable family structure, stimulates the development of many skills, gives birth to foresight and reason, the institution of private property, and trade and "knowledge of good and evil."

With respect to music and painting, Rousseau attacks a reductionist aesthetic that tends to treat these arts in terms of a sterile, mechanical analysis of the elements of products. By contrast, he emphasizes what he considers to be the crucial role of "form"—that is, of drawing in art and melody in music, for he considers both, along with language, to be meaningful only through imitation or representation. Painting is directly representative of external objects, while melody indirectly represents and evokes feelings such as joy and sorrow.

In the final chapter, Rousseau sketches briefly a remarkable distinction between liberal and slavish languages. The latter favor authoritarian obscurantism; but he suggests further that one *could* not speak clearly in, say, the King's French. Although he sarcastically exaggerates it while failing to develop it, this distinction is an important variation on the theme that languages develop according to forms of life.

J.M.

Johann Gottfried Herder

ESSAY
on the
ORIGIN OF LANGUAGE

Translated by
ALEXANDER GODE

SECTION ONE

[handwritten: separate]

[handwritten: Schon als Tier hat der Mensch Sprache. Already as an animal man has long.]

While still an animal, man already has language. All
violent sensations of his body, and among the violent the
most violent, those which cause him pain, and all strong
passions of his soul express themselves directly in screams,
in sounds, in wild inarticulate tones. A suffering animal,
no less than the hero Philoctetus, will whine, will moan
when pain befalls it, even though it be abandoned on a
desert island, without sight or trace or hope of a helpful
fellow creature. It is as though it could breathe more
freely as it vents its burning, frightened spirit. It is as
though it could sigh out part of its pain and at least draw
in from the empty air space new strength of endurance
as it fills the unhearing winds with its moans. So little
did nature create us as severed blocks of rock, as egotistic
monads! Even the most delicate chords of animal feeling
—I must use this image because I know none better for
the mechanics of sentient bodies—even the chords whose
sound and strain do not arise from choice and slow de-
liberation, whose very nature the probing of reason has
not as yet been able to fathom, even they—though there
be no awareness of sympathy from outside—are aligned
in their entire performance for a going out toward other
creatures. The plucked chord performs its natural duty:
it sounds! It calls for an echo from one that feels alike,
even if none is there, even if it does not hope or expect
that such another might answer.

Should physiology ever progress to a point where it

can demonstrate psychology—which I greatly doubt—it would derive many a ray of light for this phenomenon, though it might also divide it in individual, excessively small, and obtuse filaments. Let us accept it at present as a whole, as a shining law of nature: "Here is a sentient being which can enclose within itself none of its vivid sensations; which must, in the very first moment of surprise, utter each one aloud, apart from all choice and purpose." It was, as it were, the last motherly touch of the formative hand of nature that it gave to all, to take out into the world, the law, "Feel not for yourself alone. But rather: your feeling resound!" And since this last creative touch was, for all of one species, of one kind, this law became a blessing: "The sound of your feeling be of one kind to your species and be thus perceived by all in compassion as by one!" Do not now touch this weak, this sentient being. However lonesome and alone it may seem to be, however exposed to every hostile storm of the universe, yet is it not alone: It stands allied with all nature! Strung with delicate chords; but nature hid sounds in these chords which, when called forth and encouraged, can arouse other beings of equally delicate build, can communicate, as though along an invisible chain, to a distant heart a spark that makes it feel for this unseen being. These sighs, these sounds are language. There is, then, a language of feeling which is— underived—a law of nature.

That man has such a language, has it originally and in common with the animals, is nowadays evident, to be sure, more through certain remains than through full-fledged manifestations. But these remains, too, are incontrovertible. However much we may want to insist that our artful language has displaced the language of nature, that our civilized way of life and our social urbanity have dammed in, dried out, and channeled off the torrent and the ocean of our passions, the most violent moment of feeling—wherever, however rarely, it may occur—still time and again reclaims its right, sounding in its maternal language, without mediation, through accents. The surging storm of a passion, the sudden onslaught of joy or pleasure, pain or distress, which cut deep furrows into the soul, an overpowering feeling of revenge, despair, rage, horror, fright, and so forth, they all announce themselves, each differently after its kind. As many modes of sensitivity as are slumbering in our nature, so many tonal modes too.—And thus I note that the less human nature is akin to an animal species, the more the two differ in their nervous structures, the less shall we find the natural language of that animal species comprehensible to us. We, as animals of the earth, understand the animal of the earth better than the creature of the waters; and on the earth, the herd animal better than the creature of the forest; and among the herd animals, those best that stand closest to us. Though in the case of these latter, contact and custom too contribute their greater or lesser share. It is natural that the Arab, who is of one piece with his horse, understands it better than a man who mounts a horse for the first time—almost as well as Hector in the Iliad was able to speak with the ones that were his. The Arab in the desert, who sees no life about except his camel and perhaps a flight of erring birds, can more easily understand the camel's nature and imagine that he understands the cry of the birds than we in our dwellings. The son of the forest, the hunter, understands the voice of the hart, and the Lapp that of his reindeer—. But all that follows logically or is an exception. The rule remains that this language of nature is a group language for the members of each species among themselves. And thus man too has a language of nature all his own.

Now, to be sure, these tones are very simple, and when

they are articulated and spelled out on paper as interjections, the most contrary sensations may have almost a single expression. A dull "ah!" is as much the sound of languid love as of sinking despair; the fiery "oh!" as much the outburst of sudden joy as of boiling rage, of rising awe as of surging commiseration. But are these sounds meant to be marked down on paper as interjections? The tear which moistens this lusterless and extinguished, this solace-starved eye—how moving is it not in the total picture of a face of sorrow. Take it by itself and it is a cold drop of water. Place it under the microscope, and —I do not care to learn what it may be there. This weary breath—half a sigh—which dies away so movingly on pain-distorted lips, isolate it from its living helpmeets, and it is an empty draft of air. Can it be otherwise with the sounds of feeling? In their living contexts, in the total picture of pulsating nature, accompanied by so many other phenomena, they are moving and sufficient unto themselves. Severed from everything else, torn away, deprived of their life, they are, to be sure, no more than ciphers, and the voice of nature turns into an arbitrarily penciled symbol. Few in number are, it is true, the sounds of this language. But sentient nature, in so far as it suffers only mechanically, has likewise fewer chief varieties of feeling than our psychologies chalk up or invent as passions of the soul. But in that state every feeling is the more a mightily attracting bond, the less it is divided in separate threads. These sounds do not speak much, but what they speak is strong. Whether a plaintive sound bewails the wounds of the soul or of his body, whether it was fear or pain that forced out this scream, whether this soft "ah" clings to the bosom of the beloved in a kiss or in a tear—to establish all such distinctions was not the task of this language. It was to call attention to the picture as a whole. Leave it to that picture to speak for itself. That language was meant to sound, not to depict. Indeed, as the fable of Socrates has it, pain and pleasure touch. In feeling, nature shows its extremes interlinked, and what then can the language of feeling do but show such points of contact?—Now I may proceed with the application.

In all aborignal languages, vestiges of these sounds of nature are still to be heard, though, to be sure, they are not the principal fiber of human speech. They are not the roots as such; they are the sap that enlivens the roots of language.

A refined, late-invented metaphysical language, a variant—perhaps four times removed—of the original wild mother of the human race, after thousands of years of variation again in its turn refined, civilized, and humanized for hundreds of years of its life: such a language, the child of reason and of society, cannot know much or anything of the childhood of its earliest forebear. But the old, the wild languages, the nearer they are to their origin, the more they retain of it. Here I cannot yet speak of a formation of language that might to any extent be regarded as human. I can only consider the raw materials going into it. Not a single word exists for me as yet, only the sounds fit for a word of feeling. But behold! in the languages I mentioned, in their interjections, in the roots of their nouns and verbs, how much has not been retained of these sounds! The oldest Oriental languages are full of exclamations for which we peoples of latter-day cultures have nothing but gaps or obtuse and deaf miscomprehension. In their elegies—as among the savages in their burial grounds—those howling and wailing tones resound that are a continuous interjection of the language of nature; in their psalms of praise, the shouts for joy

and the recurrent hallelujahs, which Shaw explains from
the mouths of lamenting women and which, with us, are
so often solemn nonsense. In the flow and the rhythm
of the poems and songs of other ancient peoples echoes
the tone which still animates the dances of war and of
religion, the songs of mourning and the songs of joy of
all savages, whether they live at the foot of the Andes or
in the snows of the Iroquois, in Brazil or on the Carib-
bean Islands. The roots of the simplest, most effective
among their earliest verbs are, finally, those initial exclamations of nature, which came to be molded only at
a later time; which explains why the languages of all the
old and all the savage peoples are forever—in this inner
living tone—outside the powers of enunciation of the for-
eign-born.

The explanation of most of these phenomena must
wait for a later context. Here I note only this: One of
the upholders of the divine origin of language[1] discerns
and admires divine order in the fact that all the sounds
of all the languages known to us can be reduced to some
twenty odd letters. Unfortunately the fact is wrong, and
the conclusion still wronger. There is no language whose
living tones can be totally reduced to letters, let alone
to twenty. All languages—one and all—bear witness to
this fact. The modes of articulation of our speech organs
are so numerous. Every sound can be pronounced in so
many ways that for instance Lambert in the second part
of his Organon has been able to demonstrate, and rightly
so, how we have far fewer letters than sounds and how
imprecise therefore the latter's expression by the former

---

[1] Süssmilch, *Beweis, dass der Ursprung der Menschlichen Sprache
Göttlich sey* [*Proof that the Origin of the Language of Man Is Divine*], Berlin, 1766, p. 21.

must needs remain. And that demonstration was done only for German—a language that has not even begun to accept into its written form the differences and multiplicity of tones of its dialects. What then, when the whole language is nothing but such a living dialect? What explains all the peculiarities, all of the idiosyncrasies of orthography if not the awkward difficulty of writing as one speaks? What living language can be learned in its tones from bookish letters? And hence what dead language can be called to life? The more alive a language is—the less one has thought of reducing it to letters, the more spontaneously it rises to the full unsorted sounds of nature—the less, too, is it writeable, the less writeable in twenty letters; and for outsiders, indeed, often quite unpronounceable.

Father Rasles, who spent ten years among the Abnaki in North America, complained bitterly that with the greatest care he would often not manage to repeat more than one half of a word and was laughed at. How much more laughable would it have been for him to spell out such an expression with his French letters? Father Chaumont, who spent fifty years among the Hurons and who took on the task of writing a grammar of their language, still complained about their guttural letters and their unpronounceable accents: "Often two words consisting entirely of the same letters had the most different meanings." Garcilaso de la Vega complained that the Spaniards distorted, mutilated, and falsified the Peruvian language in the sounds of its words, attributing to the Peruvians the most dreadful things in consequence of nothing but errors of rendition. De la Condamine says of a small nation living on the Amazon River: "Some of their words could not be written, not even most imperfectly. One would need at least nine or ten syllables where in their

pronunciation they appear to utter hardly three." And
la Loubere of the language of Siam: "Of ten words pronounced by a European, a native Siamese understands
perhaps no single one, try as one may to express their
language in our letters."

But why go to peoples in such remote corners of the
world? What little we have left of savage peoples of
Europe, the Estonians and the Lapps and their like have
sounds which in many cases are just as half articulated
and unwriteable as those of the Hurons and the Peruvians. The Russians and the Poles—however long their
languages may have been written and molded by writing
—still aspirate to such an extent that the true tone of
their sounds cannot be depicted by letters. And the
Englishman, how he struggles to write his sounds, and
how little is one a speaking Englishman when one understands written English! The Frenchman, who draws
up less from the throat, and that half Greek, the Italian,
who speaks as it were in a higher region of the mouth,
in a more refined ether, still retains a living tone. His
sounds must remain within the organs where they are
formed: As drawn characters they are—however convenient and uniform long usage in writing has made
them—no more than mere shadows!

Thus the fact is wrong and the conclusion wronger:
It does not lead to a divine but—quite on the contrary
—to an animal origin. Take the so-called divine, the
first language, Hebrew, of which the greater part of the
world has inherited its letters: That in its beginnings it
was so full of living sounds that it could be written only
most imperfectly, is made quite evident by the entire
structure of its grammar, its frequent confusion of
similar letters, and especially the total lack of vowels in
it. What explains this peculiarity that its letters are ex-

clusively consonants and that precisely those elements of
the words on which everything depends, the self-sounding
vowels, were originally not written at all? This manner
of writing is so contrary to the course of sound reason
—of writing the nonessential and omitting the essential—
that it would be incomprehensible to the grammarians,
if the grammarians were accustomed to comprehend.
With us, vowels are the first, the most vital things, the
hinges of language, as it were. With the Hebrews, they
are not written. Why? Because they could not be written.
Their pronunciation was so alive and finely articulated,
their breath so spiritual and etherlike that it evaporated
and eluded containment in letters. It was only with the
Greeks that these living aspirations were pinned down in
formal vowels, though these still required a seconding
by the spiritus signs and the like, whereas with the
Orientals speech as it were was a continuous breath,
nothing but spiritus, the spirit of the mouth—as they so
often call it in their depictive poems. What the ear caught
was the breath of God, was wafting air; and the dead
characters they drew out were only the inanimate body
which the act of reading had to animate with the spirit
of life.

This is not the place to speak about the tremendous
importance of such facts for an understanding of their
language, but that this wafting reveals the origin of their
language is evident. What is more unwriteable than the
inarticulate sounds of nature? And if it is true that language is the more inarticulate the nearer it is to its
origins, it follows—does it not?—that it was surely not
invented by some superior being to fit the twenty-four
letters which were invented together with it, that these
letters were a much later and only imperfect attempt to
provide memory with a few markers, and that language

did not arise from the letters of a grammar of God but from the untutored sounds of free organs.[2] Otherwise it would be strange that precisely the letters from which and for which God invented language, by means of which He taught language to the earliest of men, are the most imperfect in the world, that they reveal nothing of the spirit of language but admit through their entire structure that they are not trying to reveal anything of it.

Judged by its worth, this hypothesis of letters would merit no more than a hint, but because of its ubiquity and the numerous attempts to cover up its shortcomings I had to unmask its baselessness and simultaneously show therein a peculiarity for which I for one know no explanation. But let us resume our course:

Since our sounds are destined to serve nature in the expression of passion, it is natural that they appear as the elements of all emotion. Who is he who—in the presence of a convulsive whimpering victim of torment, at the bedside of a moaning fellow in the throes of death, or even before a wheezing beast—when the entire machinery of the body suffers—does not feel how this Ah touches his heart? Who is so unfeeling a barbarian? The more, even in animals, the sensitive chords are strung in harmony with those of others, the more do even they feel with one another. Their nerves are tense in unison, their souls vibrate in unison, they really share with one another the mechanics of suffering. And what fibers of steel, what power to plug all inlets of sensibility are needed for a man to be deaf and hard against this!— Diderot thinks that those born blind must be less re-

---

[2] The best book on this matter, which so far has not been worked out in all its parts, is Wachter's *Naturae et scripturae concordia* [*Concordance of Nature and Scripture*], Hafn. 1752, which differs from the dreams of Kircher and numerous others as a history of antiquity differs from fairy tales.

ceptive to the plaints of a suffering animal than those who can see.[3] But I believe that in certain cases the very opposite is true. To be sure, the entire moving spectacle of this wretched convulsing creature is hidden from the blind, but all examples indicate that precisely through this concealment the sense of hearing becomes less diffuse, more pointed, and more powerfully penetrating. So there the blind man listens in darkness, in the quiet of his eternal night, and every plaintive tone, like an arrow, goes the more keenly, the more penetratingly to his heart. And now let him use the help of his slowly scanning tactile sense, let him touch the convulsions, experience in direct contact the collapse of the suffering machinery—horror and pain cut through the organs of his body; his inner nerve structure senses in resonance the collapse and the destruction; the tone of death sounds. Such is the bond of this language of nature!

Despite their cultured forms and malformation, Europeans have everywhere been keenly touched by the crude sounds of lamentation of the savages. Leri relates from Brazil how much his men were softened and moved to tears by the heartfelt, inarticulate screams of affection and good will of these Americans. Charlevoix and others do not find words enough to describe the terrifying impression made by the songs of war and magic of the North Americans. When, in a later passage, we take occasion to observe to what extent early poetry and music were inspired by these tones of nature, we shall be in a position to explain more philosophically the effect exerted on all savages, for instance, by the oldest Greek songs and dances, the old Greek stage, and music, dance, and poetry in general. And even with us, where reason to be sure often displaces emotion, where the sounds of

---

[3] *Lettres sur les aveugles: à l'usage de ceux qui voyent,* etc. [*Letters on the Blind, for the Use of Those Who See*].

nature are dispossessed by the artificial language of society—do not with us to the highest thunders of rhetoric,
the mightiest bolts of poetry, and the magic moments of
action come close to this language of nature by imitating
it? What is it that works miracles in the assemblies of
people, that pierces hearts, and upsets souls? Is it intellectual speech and metaphysics? Is it similes and figures
of speech? Is it art and coldly convincing reason? If
there is to be more than blind frenzy, much must happen
through these; but everything? And precisely this highest
moment of blind frenzy, through what did it come about?
—Through a wholly different force! These tones, these
gestures, those simple melodious continuities, this sudden turn, this dawning voice—what more do I know?—
They all—with children, with those who live through
their senses, with women, with people of sensitive feelings, with the sick, the lonely, the sorrowful—they all
accomplish a thousand times more than truth itself, even
though her soft and tender voice were sounding down
from Heaven. The words, the tone, the turn of this grue-
some ballad or the like touched our souls when we heard
it for the first time in our childhood with I know not
what host of connotations of shudder, awe, fear, fright,
joy. Speak the word, and like a throng of ghosts those
connotations arise of a sudden in their dark majesty from
the grave of the soul: They obscure inside the word the
pure limpid concept that could be grasped only in their
absence. But take the word away, and the sound of
sentiment sounds on. Dark emotion overwhelms us;
the frivolous tremble and shudder—not in reaction to
thoughts but to syllables, to the sounds of childhood;
and it was the magic power of the orator, of the poet,
that returned us to being children. No plan aforethought,
no pondered program, a straight law of nature was the

basis: "The tone of sensation shall transpose the sympathizing creature into the same tone!"

In so far as we may call these immediate sounds of sensation language, I do indeed find their origin most natural. It is not only not superhuman but obviously animal in origin: The natural law of a mechanism endowed with feelings.

But I cannot conceal my amazement that philosophers —people, that is, who look for clear concepts—ever conceived of the idea that the origin of human language might be explained from these outcries of the emotions: for is not this obviously something quite different? All animals, down to the mute fish, sound their sensations. But this does not change the fact that no animal, not even the most perfect, has so much as the faintest beginning of a truly human language. Mold and refine and organize those outcries as much as you wish; if no reason is added, permitting the purposeful use of that tone, I do not see how after the foregoing law of nature there can ever be human language—a language of volitional speech. Children, like animals, utter sounds of sensation. But is not the language they learn from other humans a totally different language?

The Abbé Condillac[4] belongs in this group. Either he supposes the whole thing called language to have been invented prior to the first page of his book, or I find things on every page that could not possibly have occurred in the orderly continuity of a language in formation. He assumes as the basis for his hypothesis "two children in a desert before they know the use of any sign." Why now he assumes all this, "two children," who

---

[4] *Essai sur l'origine des connoissances humaines* [*Essay on the Origin of Human Knowledge*], Vol. II.

must perish or turn into animals; "in a dessert," where the
difficulties opposing their survival and their inventiveness
are greatly increased; "before the use of every natural
sign"; and, to boot, "before any knowledge thereof," with
which no infant dispenses just a few weeks after its birth;
the reason—I say—that such unnatural and mutually contradictory conditions must be assumed in an hypothesis
meant to trace the natural development of human knowledge, the author of that hypothesis may or may not know;
but that what is built on it is no explanation of the origin
of language I believe I am able to prove. Condillac's two
children get together without the knowledge of any sign,
and—lo!—from the first moment on (§2) we find them
engaged in a mutual exchange. And yet it is only through
this mutual exchange that they learn "to associate with
the outcry of emotions the thoughts whose natural signs
they are." Learning natural signs of the emotions through
a mutual exchange? Learning what thoughts are associated with them? And yet being involved in an exchange
from the first moment of contact on, even before the
acquisition of a knowledge of what the dumbest animal
knows, and being able to learn—under such conditions—
what thoughts are to be associated with certain signs?
Of all this I understand nothing. "Through the recurrence
of similar circumstances (§3) they become accustomed
to associate thoughts with the sounds of the emotions
and the various signs of the body. Already their memory
is exercised. Already they have dominion over their
imagination—have advanced far enough to do by reflection what heretofore they did only by instinct" (yet, as
we just saw, did not know how to do before their exchange). Of all this I understand nothing. "The use of
these signs extends the soul's range of action (§4), and
the extended range of action of it perfects the signs:
outcries of their emotions were thus (§5) what evolved

the powers of their souls; outcries of their emotions what gave them the habit of associating ideas with arbitrary signs (§6); outcries of their emotions what served them as models in making for themselves a new language, in articulating new sounds, in becoming accustomed to designate things with names." I repeat all these repetitions, and I do not understand the first thing about them. Finally—after the author has built on this childish origin of language the prosody, declamation, music, dance, and poetry of the ancient languages, making from time to time sound observations (which, however, have nothing to do with our objective), he again takes up the thread: "In order to understand (§80) how men agreed amongst themselves on the meaning of the first words they intended to use, it suffices to remember that they uttered them under circumstances where everyone was obliged to associate them with the same ideas, etc." In short, words arose because words had arisen before they arose. Methinks it will not pay to follow further the thread of our guide for it appears to be tied—to nothing.

Condillac, with his hollow explanation of the origin of language, provided Rousseau, as we all know, with the occasion to get the question in our century off the ground again in his own peculiar way, that is, to doubt it.[5] Actually, to cast doubt on Condillac's explanation, no Rousseau was needed; but to deny straightway—because of it—all human possibility of the invention of language, that to be sure did require a little Rousseauesque verve or nerve or whatever one may wish to call it. Because Condillac had explained the thing badly, could it therefore not be explained at all? Because sounds of emotion will never turn into a human language, does it follow that nothing else could ever have turned into it?

---

[5] *Sur l'inégalité parmi les hommes,* etc. [*On the Inequality among Men*], Part I.

That it was really only this hidden fallacy which misled Rousseau is evident from his own plan: "How language would have had to originate if it is to have originated at all by human means." [6] He begins, as his predecessor did, with the outcries of nature from which human language was to arise. I shall never be able to see how language could have arisen in this way and am astonished that the acuity of a Rousseau could allow it for one moment to arise in that way.

Maupertuis' little essay is not available to me. But if I may trust the excerpts of a man among whose merits reliability and precision were not the least,[7] he too did not sufficiently differentiate the origin of language from those animal sounds. He thus walks the same road with those already mentioned.

As for Diodorus and Vitruvius finally, who—to boot—not so much derived as believed in the human origin of language, they spoiled the matter more obviously than any of the others, in that they first had men, for ages on end, roam the forests as animals with the ability to scream and then invent for themselves language, God knows from what, God knows for what.

Since now most protagonists of the human origin of language have been fighting from so shaky a position, which others—Süssmilch for instance—could attack on so many grounds, the Academy, seeing that this question (with regard to which even some of its past members differed) was still largely unanswered, wished to remove it once and for all from further controversy.

And since this great subject promises such rewarding insights into the psychology and the natural order of the human race and into the philosophy of language and of

---

[6] *Ibid.*

[7] Süssmilch, *Beweis für die Göttlichheit,* etc. [*Proof for the Divinity*], Appendix III, p. 110.

all knowledge to be found by means of language, who would not wish to try his hand at it?

And since men are for us the only creatures endowed with language that we know and since it is precisely through language that they distinguish themselves from all animals, from where could one set out more safely on the road of this investigation than from the experiences we have about the difference between the animals and men? —Condillac and Rousseau had to err in regard to the origin of language because they erred, in so well known a way and yet so differently, in regard to this difference: in that the former[8] turned animals into men and the latter[9] men into animals. I must, therefore, broaden the base of the discussion somewhat.

It seems assured that man is by far inferior to the animals in the intensity and reliability of his instincts and indeed that he does not have at all what in many animal species we regard as innate artifactive skills and drives. However, as the explanation of these drives—as handled by most writers, including quite recently one of Germany's most thorough philosophers[10]—has not been successful, so the true cause of the absence of these drives in human nature can likewise not as yet have been presented in its true light. It seems to me that one major point of view has been overlooked from which, if not complete explanations, at least insights into the nature of animals can be obtained and that these, as I hope to show in another context, may contribute greatly to clear-

---

[8] *Traité sur les animaux.*
[9] *Sur l'origine de l'inégalité,* etc.
[10] Reimarus, *Über die Kunsttriebe der Thiere* [*On the Artifactive Drives of Animals*]. See reflections on this in the *Briefe die neueste Litteratur betreffend,* etc. [*Letters Concerning the Most Recent Literature*].

ing up human psychology. The point of view I refer to
is the sphere of the animals.

Every animal has its sphere to which it belongs from
birth, into which it is born, in which it stays throughout
its life, and in which it dies; and it is a remarkable fact
that the keener the senses of the animals and the more
wonderful their artifacts, the narrower is their sphere;
the more uniform is their artifact. I have followed this
relation and I find everywhere a remarkably observed
inverse proportion of the restricted extension of their
movements, habitats, food supply, maintenance, copulation, rearing, and social behavior and their drives and
artifactive skills. The bee in its hive builds with a wisdom that Egeria could not teach her Numa; but away
from these cells and away from its predetermined activity
in these cells, the bee is nothing. The spider weaves with
the skill of Minerva, but all its skill is woven into this
narrow spider space. That is its world. How marvelous
is this insect, and how narrow the sphere of its activity.

Contrariwise. The more varied the activities and the
tasks of an animal, the more diffuse its attention and the
more numerous the objects of it, the more unsteady its
way of life, in short, the wider and the more varied its
sphere, the more we note that the power of its senses
is dispersed and weakened. I cannot permit myself here
to document with examples this great correlation which
runs through the chain of all living beings. I leave the
test to those who wish to make it, or refer to another
occasion, and proceed with my argument.

In all probability and by analogy therefore, all artifactive drives and artifactive skills of the animals can be
explained through their conceptive powers without the
need for assuming blind determinisms (of the kind still
assumed even by Reimarus and which play havoc with
all philosophy). When infinitely fine senses are concen-

trated in a narrow sphere on the same kind of object while all the rest of the world means nothing to them, how they must penetrate! When conceptive powers are locked up in a narrow sphere and are endowed with an analogous power of the senses, how they must be effective! And when finally senses and conceptions are concentrated on a single point, what else can result but instinct? From these therefore derives the explanation of the sensitivity, of the skills, and the drives of the animals in accordance with their species and their stages.

And so I may assume the postulate: The sensitivity, the skills, and the artifactive drives of the animals increase in strength and intensity in inverse proportion to the magnitude and multifariousness of their sphere of activity. But now—

Man has no such uniform and narrow sphere where only one performance is expected of him: A whole world of ventures and tasks is lying about him.

His senses and his organization are not focused on one object: He has senses for all things and hence naturally weaker and duller senses for each one.

The powers of his soul are spread over the world; there is no orientation of his conceptions toward one single object and hence no artifactive drive, no artifactive skill—and (a point which belongs most particularly in this context) no animal language.

What, in some animal species, we call language—in so far as it exceeds the aforementioned sounds produced by a machine endowed with feeling—what is it other than a result of the things listed in this series of comments, other than a vague sensuous accord among the members of an animal species with regard to their tasks inside their sphere of activity?

The narrower the sphere of an animal, the less its need for language. The keener its senses, the more clearly

focused on one object its conceptions, the more com-
pelling its drives: the more contracted is the mutual
comprehension of its possible sounds, signs, and utterances. It is a living mechanism, a ruling instinct that
speaks and perceives. How little it has to speak to be
perceived!

Animals of the narrowest sphere are consequently even
without hearing. For their world they are all eye or smell
or touch: all uniform image, uniform endeavor, uniform
performance. They thus have little or no language.

On the other hand, the more extensive the sphere of
an animal; the more differentiated its senses—but why
repeat myself? In man the setting changes completely.
In his sphere of endeavors, though it be in the poorest
of conditions, what good would be to him the language
of the most speaking, of the most multifariously sounding animal? With his dispersed appetites, his divided
attention, his more obtusely sensing senses, what good
would be to him the dark language of even all animals?
It is, to him, neither rich nor clear, neither adequate in
matter nor, in form, fitting to his organs—it just is not his
language: for what, unless we are content with playing
with words, can be meant by asserting that a language is a
language peculiar to one being than that it is appropriate
to that being's sphere of needs and endeavors, to the organization of its senses, to the orientation of its conceptions, and to the intensity of its desires—and what animal
language is that to man?

The question need hardly be asked. What language
(excepting the mechanical one spoken of before) has
man as much as a matter of instinct as every species of
animal has its own, in and after its sphere?—The answer
is short: None! And this answer in its very brevity is
decisive.

In every animal, as we have seen, its language is an

expression of such intense sensuous perceptions that these turn into instinctive drives: hence language—like senses and conceptions and instinctive drives—is congenital and directly natural to the animal. The bee hums as it sucks; the bird sings as it nests.—But how does man speak by nature? Not at all, just as he does little or nothing entirely by instinct, entirely as an animal. If in the newborn child I disregard the cries of its sensitive mechanism, it is mute. It expresses neither conceptions nor instinctive drives through sounds as any animal does in accordance with its species. And placed among animals alone, the infant is the most orphaned child of nature. Naked and bare, weak and in need, shy and unarmed: and—to make the sum of its misery complete—deprived of all guides of life. Born as it is with so dispersed, so weakened a sensuousness, with such indefinite, dormant abilities, with such divided and tired drives, clearly dependent upon a thousand needs, destined to belong to a great circle—and yet so orphaned and abandoned as not to be endowed with a language enabling it to voice its wants—No! Such a contradiction is not nature's way. In lieu of instincts, other hidden forces must be dormant in it. Born mute, but—

SECTION TWO

No, I am not jumping ahead. I do not suddenly ascribe to man—as an arbitrary *qualitas occulta*—a new power providing him with the ability to create language. Instead I shall just go on searching in the aforenoted gaps and wants.

It is not possible that gaps and wants should be the distinctive trait of the human species; else nature was to man the most cruel stepmother, while to every insect she was the most loving mother. To every insect she gave whatever and however much it needed: senses to form conceptions and conceptions shaped into drives; organs for language as far as it needed them and organs to understand this language. In man everything is in the greatest disproportion—his senses and his needs, his powers and the sphere of endeavor awaiting him, his organs and his language.—We must be missing a certain intermediate link to calculate such disparate parts in the proportion.

Were we to find that link, by all analogy in nature it would make good man's loss and be peculiarly his, be the distinctive character of his race: and all reason and all fairness would require that we regard what we have found as what it is, a gift of nature, no less essential to him than instinct to the animals.

And were we to find in just that distinctive character the cause of those wants and precisely in the area of these wants—at the bottom of his great deprivation of artifactive drives—the germ of a corresponding replacement: then this fitting accord would be a genetic proof that here lies the true direction of mankind and that the human species stands above the animals not by stages of more or of less but in kind.

And were we to find in this new-found distinctive character of mankind possibly even the necessary genetic cause of the origin of a language for this new kind of being, as we found in the instincts of animals the immediate causes of a language for each species, then we have reached our goal. In that case language would become as essential to man as it is essential that he is man. I do not, it will be admitted, proceed on the basis of arbitrary or social forces but from the general animal economy.

And now it follows that if man's senses, when applied to any small area of the earth, to work and to enjoyment within a segment of the world, are inferior in acuity to the senses of the animal which lives within that segment, then it is precisely this that gives his senses the advantage of freedom. Because they are not senses for one spot, they become generalized senses for the universe.

If man has powers of conception which are not confined to the construction of a honey cell or of a cobweb and which hence are inferior to the artifactive capacities of animals within that particular sphere, it is precisely for this reason that his powers of conception achieve a wider perspective. There is no single work of man in which his actions are not improvable, but he enjoys the freedom of exercise in many things and hence the freedom of improving himself forever. A thought, any thought, is not a direct work of nature, and for that very reason it can be a work of his own.

If instinct must thus fall by the wayside, in so far as it followed exclusively from the organization of the senses and the confines of conceptions and was not determined blindly, precisely on account of this man achieves greater light. Since he does not fall blindly in any particular spot and does not lie blind in it, he learns to stand free, to find for himself a sphere of self-reflection, and seek his reflection in himself. No longer an infallible machine in the hands of nature, he himself becomes a purpose and an objective of his efforts.

Call this entire disposition of man's forces rationality, reason, reflection, call it what you will. As long as these names are not intended to stand for a particular force, or for no more than a stepped-up potentiation of animal forces, I shall not object. What it is, is the total arrangement of all human forces, the total economy of his sensuous and cognitive, of his cognitive and volitional nature, or rather: It is the unique positive power of thought which, associated with a particular organization of the body, is called reason in man as in the animal it turns into an artifactive skill; which in man is called freedom and turns in the animal into instinct. The difference is not one of degree nor one of a supplementary endowment with powers; it lies in a totally distinct orientation and evolution of all powers. Whether a man be a follower of Leibnitz or of Locke, whether his name be Search or Know-all,[1] whether he be an idealist or a materialist, he must—in consequence of the foregoing, with the assumption of a certain agreement regarding the meaning of words—admit the fact of a distinctive character of mankind which consists in this and in nothing else.

All those who have raised objections against this were deluded by wrong notions and badly organized concepts. The attempt has been made to think of man's reason as a new and totally detached power that was put into his soul and given to him before all animals as a special additional gift and which, like the fourth step of a ladder with three steps below, must be considered by itself. And that to be sure—no matter how great the philosophers were who said so—is philosophical nonsense. All the powers of our soul and those of the animals are nothing but metaphysical abstractions, effects. We separate them from the rest because our feeble minds cannot consider them at once: They appear in chapters, not because they work in nature chapter by chapter, but because an apprentice finds it easiest to develop them for himself in that fashion. If we have grouped certain activities of the soul under certain major designations,

---

[1] A division favored in a recent metaphysical treatise, *Search's Light of nature pursued*, London, 1768.

such as wit, perspicacity, fantasy, reason, this does not
mean that a single act of the mind is ever possible in
which only wit or only reason is at work; it means no
more than that we discern in that act a prevailing share
of the abstraction which we call wit or reason, as for
instance the comparison or the elucidation of ideas; yet
in everything the total undivided soul is at work. If ever
a man was able to perform a single act in which he
thought totally like an animal, he is *ipso facto* no longer a
man in any thing, no longer capable of any human act. If
he was for one single moment devoid of reason, I do not
see how ever in his life he could think with reason unless
it be that his entire soul, the entire economy of his nature,
underwent a change.

A sounder conception makes of man's rationality, of
this distinctive character of his species, something quite
different; it makes of it the overall determination of his
powers of thought within the total complex of his senses
and of his drives. And then, if we take all our previous
analogies into account, there is no possibility other than
that. . . .

If man had the drives of the animals, he could not
have what we now call reason in him; for such drives
would pull his forces darkly toward a single point, in
such a way that he would have no free sphere of awareness. There is only the possibility that. . . .

If man had the senses of the animals, he would have
no reason; for the keen alertness of his senses and the
mass of perceptions flooding him through them would
smother all cool reflection. But inversely, these very same
laws of balance within the economy of nature imply of
necessity that. . . .

If animal sensuousness and the animal's limitation to
a single point were omitted, another creature would have
come into being, one whose positive powers expressed

themselves in a vaster realm, after a finer organization, with greater light; one which in separation and in freedom does not achieve only knowledge, follow its will, and pursue its work, but which also knows that it achieves its work. This creature is man, and this entire disposition of his nature—in order to escape the confusion resulting from the attribution of independent powers of reason and the like—we shall call reflection. It follows then from precisely these rules of balance, since all such words as sensuousness and instinct, fantasy and reason are after all no more than determinations of one single power wherein opposites cancel each other out, that. . . .

If man was not to be an instinctual animal, he had to be—by virtue of the more freely working positive power of his soul—a creature of reflection.—And if I carry this chain of conclusions a few links further, I can achieve—in anticipation of later objections—a head start which will considerably shorten my path.

For if reason is not a separate and singly acting power but an orientation of all powers and as such a thing peculiar to his species, then man must have it in the first state in which he is man. In the first thought of the child this reflection must be apparent, just as it is apparent in the insect that it is an insect.—And this now is something which more than one author has been unable to grasp, and that is why the matter of which I write is filled with the crudest, the most nauseating interjections —but they could not grasp it, because they misunderstood it. Why, does thinking reasonably right away signify thinking with fully developed reason? Does the assertion that the infant thinks with reflection signify that it reasons like a sophist from his rostrum or a statesman in his cabinet? Happy and thrice happy that it knew nothing as yet of this tiring lumber of hair-splitting ratiocination!

But is it so hard to understand that this objection denies only a particular use of the forces of the soul, a more or less trained use which proceeds thus and so and not otherwise, and not at all the positive reality of a force of the soul as such? And what fool would maintain that man thinks from the first moment of life as after years of training—unless one denies at once the possibility of growth in all the forces of the soul and thus declares oneself by implication a mental minor?— But as such growth cannot possibly mean anything but greater ease, intensity, and multifariousness of use, it is necessarily implied—is it not?—that what is to be used must be there beforehand, that what is to grow must be there as a germ. And is not, in this sense, the whole tree present in the seed?—As little as the child has the claws of a griffon and the mane of a lion, as little can it think as griffons and lions do; but if it thinks as humans do, then reflection—that is to say, the tempering of all its powers in subservience to this major orientation— is as much its destiny at the first moment of its life as it will be at the last.

Under its sensuousness reason manifests itself with such effectiveness that the Omniscient who created this soul saw in its first state the full web of life's actions, as for instance the geometrician finds from one element in the progression, when the class is given, its full constitution.

"In that case, however, reason was at the time rather a potentiality of reason (*réflexion en puissance*) than an active power!" This objection says nothing. Pure potentiality, existing in the absence of objects not as a power but as nothing beyond potentiality, is as much a hollow sound as plastic forms which form without being forms themselves. If, together with the potentiality, there is not the slightest positive inkling of a tendency, then nothing is there—then the word is no more than a scholastic abstraction. The contemporary French philosopher,[2] who succeeded in making this sham concept of the *réflexion en puissance* so dazzling, made dazzling—as we shall see—no more than an air bubble which for a while he keeps blowing ahead of himself but which not even he can prevent from unexpectedly bursting as he proceeds along his way. And if there is nothing in the postulated potentiality, through what should it ever get into the soul? If in the first state there is no positive trace of reason in the soul, how should it ever become real in millions of subsequent states?

It is a verbal delusion that use can transform a potentiality into potency, can transform something merely possible into something real. If force is not present, it cannot be used and applied. And then finally, what are these two, an isolated rational potentiality and a separate rational force in the soul? The one is as incomprehensible as the other. Place man—as the creature which he is, with the degree of sensuousness and the organization which he has—into the universe: from all sides, through all his senses, the universe flows in upon him in his sensations. Through human senses? In a human way? Is not then this thinking, in comparison with the animals, being less flooded? And if it has room to express its powers more freely, and if this condition is called rationality—where then is mere potentiality? Where isolated power of reason? It is the positive, unique power of the soul which acts in primordial balance—the more sensuously, the less rationally; if more reasonably, then less spontaneously; if with more light, then less darkly—all that goes without saying. But in the most sensuous state, man is still human; and hence there still was in him the activity of reflection, although to a less notable degree. And the least sensuous

---

2 Rousseau, *On the Inequality*, etc.

state of the animals was still animal, and hence—with all the clarity of their thought— there never worked in them the reflection of a human concept. And beyond this let us not play with words!

I regret to have lost so much time in defining and organizing mere concepts. But it is a loss which could not be avoided, for in modern times this entire area of psychology has been turned into a pitiful wasteland because French philosophers, pursuing some seeming peculiarities in the nature of the animal and of man, have turned everything upside down, while German philosophers arrange most of these concepts more for the benefit of their systems and in accordance with their individual points of view than with the object of avoiding confusion from the standpoint of common thought. And then, in straightening out these concepts, I did not actually go out of my way, for of a sudden we find ourselves at our goal! To wit:

Man, placed in the state of reflection which is peculiar to him, with this reflection for the first time given full freedom of action, did invent language. For what is reflection? What is language?

This reflection is characteristically peculiar to man and essential to his species; and so is language and the invention of language.

Invention of language is therefore as natural to man as it is to him that he is man. Let us simply develop these two concepts further: reflection and language—

Man manifests reflection when the force of his soul acts in such freedom that, in the vast ocean of sensations which permeates it through all the channels of the senses, it can, if I may say so, single out one wave, arrest it, concentrate its attention on it, and be conscious of being attentive. He manifests reflection when, confronted with the vast hovering dream of images which pass by his

senses, he can collect himself into a moment of wakeful-
ness and dwell at will on one image, can observe it clearly
and more calmly, and can select in it distinguishing marks
for himself so that he will know that this object is this
and not another. He thus manifests reflection if he is able
not only to recognize all characteristics vividly or clearly
but if he can also recognize and acknowledge to himself
one or several of them as distinguishing characteristics.
The first act of this acknowledgment[3] results in a clear
concept; it is the first judgment of the soul—and through
what did this acknowledgment occur? Through a distinguishing mark which he had to single out and which,
as a distinguishing mark for reflection, struck him clearly.
Well, then! Let us acclaim him with shouts of eureka!
This first distinguishing mark, as it appeared in his reflection, was a work of the soul! With it human language is
invented!

Let that lamb there, as an image, pass by under his
eyes; it is to him, as it is to no other animal. Not as it
would appear to the hungry, scenting wolf! Not as it
would appear to the blood-lapping lion.—They scent and
taste in anticipation! Sensuousness has overwhelmed them.
Instinct forces them to throw themselves over it.—Not as
it appears to the rutting ram which feels it only as the object of its pleasure, which thus—again—is overcome by
sensuousness, and which—again—is forced by instinct to
throw itself over it.—Not as it appears to any other animal to which the sheep is indifferent and which therefore
lets it, clear-darkly, pass by because its instinct makes it
turn toward something else!—Not so with man! As soon
as he feels the need to come to know the sheep, no in-

---

[3] One of the most beautiful treatises to illuminate the nature of
apperception on the basis of physical experiments (which only
rarely serve to elucidate the metaphysics of the soul) is to be found
in the publications of the Berlin Academy of 1764.

stinct gets in his way; no one sense of his pulls him too close to it or too far away from it. It stands there, entirely as it manifests itself in his senses. White, soft, woolly— his soul in reflective exercise seeks a distinguishing mark —the sheep bleats! His soul has found the distinguishing mark. The inner sense is at work. This bleating, which makes upon man's soul the strongest impression, which broke away from all the other qualities of vision and of touch, which sprang out and penetrated most deeply, the soul retains it. The sheep comes again. White soft, woolly —the soul sees, touches, remembers, seeks a distinguishing mark—the sheep bleats, and the soul recognizes it. And it feels inside, "Yes, you are that which bleats." It has recognized it humanly when it recognized and named it clearly, that is, with a distinguishing mark. More darkly? In that case it would not have perceived it at all, because no sensuousness, no instinct relative to the sheep could replace for it the lack of distinctness with a more vivid clarity. Distinctly and directly but without a distinguishing mark? In that way no sensuous being can perceive outside itself, for there are forever other feelings which it must repress, annihilate as it were, in order to recognize, as it forever must, the difference between one and another through a third. Thus through a distinguishing mark? And what was that other than a distinguishing word within? The sound of bleating perceived by a human soul as the distinguishing mark of the sheep became, by virtue of this reflection, the name of the sheep, even if his tongue had never tried to stammer it. He recognized the sheep by its bleating: This was a conceived sign through which the soul clearly remembered an idea —and what is that other than a word? And what is the entire human language other than a collection of such words? Even if the occasion were never to arise for him that he should want or be able to transmit this idea to

another being, and thus to bleat out with his lips this
distinguishing mark of reflection for another, his soul—
as it were—bleated within when it selected this sound as
a sign of recollection, and it bleated again as it recognized
the sound by its sign. Language has been invented! Invented as naturally and to man as necessarily as man
was man.

Most of those who have written about the origin of
language did not look for it here which is the only place
where it could be found. And many have therefore been
in the throes of innumerable dark doubts as to whether
it might be found anywhere within the human soul. It
has been looked for in the superior articulation of the
organs of speech. As if ever an orangutan with precisely
the same organs had invented a language. It has been
looked for in the sounds of passion. As though it were
not true that all animals have these sounds and as though
any animal had invented language from them. It has been
assumed to be a basic principle that man wants to imitate
nature and hence also nature's sounds. As though such a
blind inclination had any room for thought. And as
though the ape with precisely this inclination, or the
blackbird which is so well able to mimic sounds, had
invented a language. Most, finally, have assumed a mere
convention, an agreement, and against this Rousseau has
spoken the most vehemently, for what an obscure and involved term is this, a natural agreement of language?
These numerous unbearable fallacies that have been
stated in support of the human origin of language finally
made the opposite view almost universal—though I do
not hope that it will remain so. The point here is that it
is not an organization of the mouth that made language,
for even one who is mute for life, if he is human and if he
reflects, has language lying in his soul. The point here is
that it is not a scream of emotion, for not a breathing

machine but a reflective being invented language. Not a principle of imitation in the soul, for what there is of imitation of nature is merely a means to an end, the one end that is here to be explained. Least of all is it agreement, an arbitrary convention of society. The savage, the hermit living alone in the forest, would have had to invent language for himself, even though he had never spoken it. It was an agreement of his soul with itself and so necessary an agreement as it is necessary that man is man. If others found it incomprehensible how a human soul could invent language, to me it is incomprehensible how a human soul could be what it is and not, by that fact alone—without the help of a mouth and without the presence of a society —be led to invent language.

Nothing can serve to elaborate this origin more clearly than the objections of the opponents. The most thorough, the most comprehensive defender of the divine origin of language[4]—precisely because he looked below the surface which the others barely touched—almost turns into a defender of the true human origin. He stopped at the very threshold of the proof, and his major objection, if explained slightly more correctly, turns into an objection against himself and into a proof of the opposite, the human possibility of language. He believes to have demonstrated "that the use of language is necessary for the use of reason." If he had done so, I do not know what else would thus be demonstrated but "that, since the use of reason is natural to man, the use of language must be so, too." Unfortunately, however, he did not prove his postulate. He only explained laboriously that all the delicate and complex actions which we call attention, reflection, abstraction, etc., cannot very well be performed without signs to lend the soul support. However, this "not very

---

[4] Süssmilch, *op. cit.*, Section 2.

well," "not easily," "not likely," does not go to the end of it
all. As we, with our limited powers of abstraction, can
think only a small amount of abstraction without sensual
signs, so other beings may be able to think a greater
amount of it without them. In any event, it does not follow at all that in and by itself no abstraction is possible
without a sensual sign. I have demonstrated that the use
of reason is not only "not very well" possible without signs
but that not even the least use of reason, not even the
simplest distinct recognition, not the most primitive judgment of human reflection is possible without a distinguishing mark, for the difference between one and another can
never be recognized through anything but a third. Precisely this third, this characteristic mark, becomes thus an
inner characteristic word: so that language follows quite
naturally from the initial act of reason.—Süssmilch[5] un-
dertook to show that the higher applications of reason
are not possible without language, and to that end he
quoted Wolf who, however, does no more in this matter
than speak in probabilities. Strictly speaking the point is
irrelevant, for the higher applications of reason, which do
have a place in the speculative areas of man's pursuit of
knowledge, were after all not necessary in the laying
of the first cornerstone of language.—And yet, even this
easily demonstrated postulate has not been demonstrated
but only discussed by Süssmilch, while I believe I have
demonstrated that not even the first and most primitive
application of reason was possible without language. But
if he now argues on: no man can have invented language
for himself because reason was necessary for the very
invention of language so that language would have had to
be present before it was present—then I stop the perpetual merry-go-round, look at it more closely, and now it

---

[5] *Ibid.*, p. 49.

signifies something quite different: *ratio et oratio!* If reason was not possible to man without language, well! then
the invention of the latter is to man as natural, as old, as
original, as characteristic as the use of the former.

I have called Süssmilch's manner of arguing a perpetual merry-go-round, for I can turn it as well against him as
he can turn it against me, and the thing goes round and
round forever. Without language man has no reason,
and without reason no language. Without language and
reason he is not capable of receiving divine instruction,
and without divine instruction he has neither reason nor
language. Where shall this lead to? How can man acquire
language through divine instruction if he lacks reason?
And he has not the slightest use of reason without language. He therefore is to have language before he has it
and can have it? Or be able to be rational without having
the least use of a power of reason of his own? To be able
to acquire the first syllable of divine instruction, he had
to be—as Süssmilch himself admits—a human being, that
is, be able to think clearly, and when he conceived the
first clear thought, language was already present in his
soul, being there through his own resources and not invented through divine instruction.—I well know what
those who speak of divine instruction normally have in
mind. They think of the language instruction which parents give their children. But if we reflect, we see that this
is not our case at all. Parents never teach their children
language without the latter, by themselves, inventing language along with them: Parents merely draw their children's attention to differences between things by means
of certain verbal signs, and consequently they do not replace, but only facilitate and promote for them, the use
of reason through language.

If for other reasons this sort of supernatural facilitation
is to be assumed, that has no bearing on my purpose;

though in that case, too, it would not by any means be God who invented language for man, but it would still be man who had to invent language for himself by means of forces of his own, albeit under a superior guidance. In order to be able to receive from the mouth of God the first word as a word, that is, as a characteristic sign of reason, man had to have reason and had to apply the same reflection to understand this word as a word as though he had thought it out himself in the first place. So then, all the arms of my adversary are fighting against him; man had to have real use of reason in order to learn divine language. And that use every learning child has, too, unless it is, like a parrot, to utter mere words without thoughts. But what sort of scholars worthy of God would they be who learned in that manner?—And if they had always learned thus, from where would we have derived our language of reason?

I flatter myself that if my worthy opponent were still alive he would see that his objection, somewhat more fully specified, turns into the strongest proof against him and that thus he himself unwittingly gathered together in his book material to disprove his own position. He would not attempt to hide behind the term "potentiality of reason which is not as yet reason in any way." For turn as one may, there arise contradictions. A creature of reason without the least use of reason, or a creature endowed with the use of reason without—language. A creature without reason which can receive instruction from reason; or a creature capable of instruction which yet has no reason. A creature wholly without the use of reason—and yet man! A being which could not use its reason through natural forces and yet learned to use it naturally in supernatural instruction. A human language which was not human at all, that is, which could not arise through human forces, and yet a language so human that without it none of the forces proper to man can manifest itself. A thing without which he was not man and yet a state in which he was man but had not that thing which hence was there before it was there, which had to manifest itself before it could manifest itself, etc.—All these contradictions are evident if man, reason, and language are taken as the reality which they are and the ghost of a word "potentiality" (the potentiality of man to be man, the potentiality of reason to be reason, the potentiality of language to be language) is unmasked in its nonsensicalness.

"But the savage human infants among the bears, did they have language? And were they not human?"[6] Surely! But they were, firstly, human in a state contrary to nature! Human in a state contrary to the human species! Put a rock on this plant: will it not grow up crooked? And is it not nonetheless, by its nature, a straight-sprouting plant? And did not its straight-sprouting force manifest itself even where it hugged deviously around that rock? And thus, secondly, the very possibility of being in a state contrary to the human species does show human nature. Precisely because man has not the relentless instincts of animals, because he has capabilities for many things, and for everything capabilities that are weaker—in short, it is because man is man that he could veer off into a degenerate state. Could he have learned to growl like a bear, could be have learned to crawl like a bear, had he not had organs that are flexible, had he not had limbs that are flexible? Would any other animal—a monkey, a donkey— have advanced that far? Was it not then in fact the action of his human nature that made it possible for him to become so unnatural? But, thirdly, despite all that, his nature remained human nature: for did he growl, crawl, eat,

---

[6] *Ibid.,* p. 48.

scent, completely like a bear? Or would he not rather
have remained forever a stumbling, a stammering man-
bear and thus an imperfect dual creature? As little, then,
as his skin and his face, as his feet and his tongue could be
changed and transformed completely into a bearish shape,
so little—let us no longer be in doubt!—could the nature
of his soul be thus changed and transformed. His reason
lay buried under the pressure of sensuousness, of bearish
instincts, but still it was human reason, for those instincts
were never completely bearish. And that this is how it
was, is shown in the end, by the outcome of the entire
story. When the obstacles were removed, when these
bear-men returned to their kin, did they not learn to stand
up and walk and to speak more naturally than they had
previously—unnaturally—to crawl and to growl? The latter they did at best *like* bears; the former they learned,
in a short space of time, to do entirely *as* men. Which of
their former sylvan brethren learned this together with
them? And since no bear could learn it because he did
not possess the requisite disposition of body and soul,
does it not follow that the man-bear maintained such
disposition throughout the state of his life away from his
species? Had it come to him through mere training and
habit, why not to the bear? And what would it mean if
someone, through training, received reason and humanity
which he did not have before? Presumably this needle
gave the eye the power of vision by couching its cataract.
What then can we infer about nature from a case which is
most unnatural? If we admit that it is an unnatural case—
well! being unnatural, it confirms nature!

Rousseau's entire hypothesis of the inequality of men is
patently built on such aberrancies, and his doubts against
the humanness of language concern either erroneous
theses of origin or the aforementioned difficulty that the
invention of language presupposes reason. As for the first,

Rousseau's doubts are right; as for the second, they have
been disproved and can be disproved through Rousseau's
own words. That phantom of his, natural man, this creature contrary to its own species, which on the one hand he
makes get along with a mere potentiality of reason, appears on the other hand endowed with perfectibility,
with perfectibility as a characteristic trait, with perfectibility to so high a degree that by means of it he can learn
from all animal species. See now what Rousseau has
granted man! More than we want and more than we need!
That first thought, "Lo! that is something peculiar to the
animal! The wolf howls! The bear growls!," that first
thought (thought in such a way that it could connect with
the second, "And howling and growling are things I have
not!"), that first thought already is true reflection. And
then in the third and fourth thoughts: "Well! That would
not go badly with my nature either! That I might emulate!
That I will emulate! Through that my kin would become
more perfect!" What a wealth of fine, concatenated reflection! Wherein the creature that was able to argue out
the first of these already had to have language of the soul!
Already had that art of thinking which produced the art
of speaking. The ape may forever be aping, but never did
he emulate. He never reflected, saying to himself, "That I
will emulate in order to perfect my kind!" For had he ever
said so, had he ever made a single act of emulation his
own, giving it permanence in his kind through choice and
intent, had he been able, just one single time, to think
one single such reflection—that very moment he ceased to
be an ape! With all his apish appearance, without a sound
from his tongue, he was an inwardly speaking human,
who sooner or later had to invent for himself an utterable language. But what orangutan, though equipped
with all human organs of speech, ever spoke a single human word?

There still are in Europe some good-natured primitivists who say, "Well yes perhaps—if the ape just wanted to speak!—or if the ape had the occasion!—or if the ape could!"—Could! That would be the most fitting, for the preceding two ifs are sufficiently ruled out through the natural history of the animal kingdom, and it is not for the lack of organs, as I have stated, that the "if it could" is stopped in its tracks.[7] The orangutan has a head, outside and inside, like ours; but did it ever speak? Parrots and starlings have learned enough human sounds; but have they ever thought a human word?—But anyway, it is not as yet the external sounds of words that concern us here; we are here concerned with the inner, the necessary genesis of a word as the characteristic mark of a distinct reflection—and when ever has an animal species, in whatever way it may have been, manifested that? Such a thread of thoughts, such a discourse of the soul, no matter what type of utterance it might use, would have to be subject to observation; but who has ever observed it? The fox has acted a thousand times as Aesop had him act, but he has never acted in Aesop's sense, and the first time that he can do that, Master Fox will invent his own language for himself and be able to fabulate about Aesop the way Aesop, as things are, did about him. The dog has learned to understand many words and commands, but not as words, only as signs associated with gestures and actions. Were he ever to understand a single word in the human sense, he would no longer serve, he would create for himself his art, his society, and his language. It is easy to see, if once the precise point of genesis has been missed, the field of error is immeasurably vast in all directions! Down

---

[7] From Camper's *Zergliederung des Orang-Outang* [*Analysis of the Orangutan*] (see his translated minor writings), it appears that this assertion was too bold. But at the time when I wrote these lines it was the generally accepted opinion among anatomists.

one way, language appears to be so superhuman that God had to invent it; down the other, it is so unhuman that every animal could invent it if it were but to take the trouble. The goal of truth is just one point! With our course set for it, we perceive to the right and the left why no animal can invent language, why no God need invent language, and why man, as man, can and must invent language.

I do not wish, on metaphysical grounds, to pursue further the hypothesis of the divine origin of language, for psychologically its baselessness has been shown in the fact that, in order to understand the language of the gods on Olympus, man must come endowed with reason and hence endowed with language. Still less can I pursue in greater detail the pleasant matter of the animal languages, for all—as we have seen—stand totally and incommensurably apart from the language of man. What I am most loathe to renounce are the diverse perspectives which, from this genetic point of language in the human soul, open out into the wide fields of logic, aesthetics, and psychology, especially with regard to the question, how far can one think without and what must one think with language, a question whose subsequent applications would spread out into practically all branches of knowledge. Here it must suffice to observe that language, from without, is the true differential character of our species as reason is from within.

In more than one language, word and reason, concept and word, language and cause have hence one designation, and this synonymy comprises their full genetic origin. Amongst the Orientals it has come to be a common turn of expression to call the recognition of a thing the naming of it: for deep in the soul the two actions are one. They call man the speaking animal and the unreasoning animals the mutes: The expression is palpably characteristic, and the Greek term *alogos* comprises both. Thus language appears as a natural organ of reason, a sense of the human soul, as the power of vision—in the story of the sensitive soul of the Ancients—built for itself the eye and the instinct of the bee builds its cell.

Excellent how this new, self-made sense of the mind is in its very origin again a means of contact!—I cannot think the first human thought, I cannot align the first reflective argument without dialoguing in my soul or without striving to dialogue. The first human thought is hence in its very essence a preparation for the possibility of dialoguing with others! The first characteristic mark which I conceive is a characteristic word for me and a word of communication for others!

Sic verba, quibus voces sensusque notarent,
Nominaque invenere—

HORACE

SECTION THREE

The focal point has been found where Prometheus' divine spark ignites in the human soul—with the first characteristic mark there was language. But what were the first characteristic marks to serve as elements of language?

I. *Sounds*

Cheselden's blind man[1] shows how slowly the sense of vision evolves, how difficult it is for the soul to establish

---

[1] *Philosophical Transactions,* abridgment. Also in *Cheselden's Anatomy,* in Smith-Kästner's optics, in Buffon's natural history, in the encyclopedia, and in a dozen small French dictionaries under the key word *"aveugle."*

the concepts of space, of form, and of color, and how
many trials are needed and what geometric art must be
acquired in order to use these characteristic marks with
clarity. That therefore was not the most appropriate of
the senses to be used in language. Furthermore, its phenomena were so cold and mute while the sensations received by the coarser senses were so indistinct and so
intermingled that, by the very nature of things, it was
either nothing or the ear that had to become the first
teacher of language.

There is for instance the sheep. As an image it looms
before the eye with all things and images and colors on a
great canvas of nature. How much is there and how difficult to distinguish! All the characteristic marks are finely
interwoven, placed together, and all still ineffable! Who
can speak shapes? Who can sound colors? Let him take
the sheep under his probing hand. This sensation is more
secure and fuller, but it is so full and so obscure, with one
thing within the other. Who can say what he is thus feeling? But listen! The sheep bleats! Now one distinguishing
mark separates by itself from the canvas of the colors
wherein so little was to be distinguished. One distinguishing mark has penetrated deeply and clearly into the soul.
"Oh," says the learning beginner, like Cheselden's blind
man when given the power of sight, "now I shall know
you again—you bleat!" The dove coos, the dog barks!
Three words have arisen because he tried three distinct
ideas. The latter go into his logic as the former into his
vocabulary. Reason and language together took a timid
step and nature came to meet them halfway—through the
power of hearing. Nature did not merely ring out the
characteristic mark, it rang it in, deep into the soul. There
was a sound, the soul grasped for it, and there it had a
ringing word.

So man is a listening, a noting creature, naturally

formed for language, and even a blind and a mute man—
we understand—would have to invent language if he is
not without feeling and is not deaf. Place him at ease and
in comfort on a deserted island: Nature will reveal itself
to him through the ear. A thousand creatures that he cannot see will still appear to speak to him, and though his
mouth and his eye remain closed forever, his soul is not
wholly without language. When the leaves of the tree
rustle refreshing coolness down upon the poor man in his
solitude, when the passing waters of the murmuring brook
rock him to sleep, when the whispering west wind fans
his burning cheeks—the bleating sheep gives him milk,
the flowing brook water, the rustling tree fruit—enough of
interest for him to *know* the beneficent beings; enough of
urgency, without eyes and without speech, for him to
name them in his soul. The tree will be called the rustler,
the west wind the fanner, the brook the murmurer—and
there, all finished and ready, is a little dictionary, waiting
for the imprint of the speech organs. But how poor and
how strange would the conceptions be which this mutilated individual could associate with such sounds![2]

But now grant man the freedom of all his senses: let
him see and touch and feel simultaneously all the beings
which speak into his ear—Heavens! What a lecture hall
of ideas and of language! Do not bother to bring down
from the clouds a Mercury or Apollo as operatic *Dei ex
machina.*—The entire, multisonant, divine nature is man's
teacher of language and man's muse. Past him it leads a
procession of all creatures: Each one has its name on its
tongue and introduces itself to this concealed yet visible
god as a vassal and servant. It delivers to him its distinguishing word to be entered, like a tribute, into the book

---

[2] Diderot in his entire letter *Sur les sourds et muets* [*On the Deaf
and Mute*] hardly got around to discussing this central point, for he
spent his time with inversions and a hundred other details.

of his dominion so that he may, by virtue of its name, remember it, call it in future, and enjoy it. I ask if ever this
truth—the truth that "the very power of reason by which
man rules over nature was the father of the living language which he abstracted from the tones of sounding
beings as characteristic marks of differentiation"—I ask
whether in the style of the Orient this sober truth could
ever be expressed more nobly and more beautifully than
in the words, "And God brought the animals unto the man
to see what he would call them; and whatsoever the man
called every living creature, that was the name thereof."
Where, in the poetic manner of the Orient, could there be
a more definite statement that man invented language for
himself—from the tones of living nature—as characteristic
marks of his ruling reason!—And that is what I prove.

If an angel or a heavenly spirit had invented language,
how could its entire structure fail to bear the imprint of
the manner of thinking of that spirit, for through what
could I know the picture of an angel in a painting if not
through its angelic and supernatural features? But where
does the like occur in our language? Structure and design
and even the earliest cornerstone of this palace reveals
humanity!

In what language are celestial and spiritual concepts
the first? Those concepts which, according to the principles of our thinking mind, too, ought to be the first—subjects, *notiones communes,* the germinal seeds of our cog-
nition, the centers about which everything revolves and
to which everything leads back—are these living centers
to be found as elements of language? It would appear
natural that the subjects should have preceded the predicates, that the simplest subjects should have preceded the
composed ones, the thing that acts and does the acts and
doings of it, essentials and certainties the uncertain and
accidental. How much more could one not conclude in

this manner, yet—in our original languages it is clearly the very opposite that holds true. A hearing, a listening creature is evident, but no celestial spirit, for—

Sounding verbs are the first elements of power. Sounding verbs? Actions and nothing as yet that acts? Predicates and no subject as yet? The celestial genius would have to blush for it but not the sensuous human being, for what— as we have seen—could move this being more profoundly than those sounding actions? And what else, after all, is the entire structure of language but a manner of growth of his spirit, a history of his discoveries? The divine origin explains nothing and allows nothing to be explained from it. It is—as Bacon said of another thing—a holy vestal, dedicated to the gods but infertile, pious but of no use!

The first vocabulary was thus collected from the sounds of the world. From every sounding being echoed its name: The human soul impressed upon it its image, thought of it as a distinguishing mark.—How could it be otherwise than that these sounding interjections came first? And so, for example, the Oriental languages are full of verbs as basic roots of the language. The thought of the thing itself was still hovering between the actor and the action: The sound had to designate the thing as the things gave forth the sound. From the verbs it was that the nouns grew and not from the nouns the verbs. The child names the sheep, not as a sheep, but as a bleating creature, and hence makes of the interjection a verb. In the gradual progress of human sensuousness, this state of affairs is explicable; but not in the logic of a higher spirit.

All the old unpolished languages are replete with this origin, and in a philosophical dictionary of the Orientals every stem word with its family—rightly placed and soundly evolved—would be a chart of the progress of the human spirit, a history of its development, and a complete dictionary of that kind would be a most remarkable sample of the inventive skill of the human soul. Also of God's method of language and of teaching? I doubt it!

Since all of nature sounds, nothing is more natural to a sensuous human being than to think that it lives, that it speaks, that it acts. That savage saw the tall tree with its mighty crown and sensed the wonder of it: the crown rustled! There the godhead moves and stirs! The savage falls down in adoration! Behold, that is the story of sensuous man, the dark link by which nouns are fashioned from verbs—and a faint move toward abstraction! With the savages of North America, for instance, everything is still animated: Every object has it genius, its spirit, and that the same held true with the Greeks and Orientals is attested by their oldest vocabulary and grammar. They are what all of nature was to their inventor: a pantheon, a realm of animated, of acting beings!

But as man referred everything to himself, as everything appeared to speak to him and indeed acted for or against him; as he thus engaged himself with or against it, as he loved or hated and conceived of everything in human terms—all these traces of humanity appear impressed in the first names! They, too, spoke love or hatred, curse or blessing, tenderness or adversity, and in particular there arose from this feeling, in many languages, the articles! Everything was personified in human terms, as woman and man. Everywhere gods, goddesses, acting beings of evil or of good. The howling storm and the sweet zephyr, the clear source and the mighty ocean— their entire mythology lies in the treasure trove, the verbs and nouns of the old languages, and the oldest dictionary was thus a sounding pantheon, an assembly of both sexes, as was nature to the senses of the first inventor. Here the language of an old unpolished nation appears as a study

in the aberrations of human fantasy and passion as does
its mythology. Every family of words is a tangled under-
brush around a sensuous central idea, around a sacred
oak, still bearing traces of the impression received by the
inventor from this dryad. Feelings are interwoven in it:
What moves is alive; what sounds speaks; and since it
sounds for or against you, it is friend or foe: god or god-
dess, acting from passion as are you!

What I love in this manner of thinking is the humanity
of it, the sensuous being in it: Everywhere I see the weak,
timid, sensitive being who must love or hate, trust or fear
and longs to spread over all existence these sensations in
his heart. I see everywhere the weak yet mighty being
that is in need of the entire universe and involves everything in war or peace with itself; that depends on everything and yet rules over everything. The poetry and the
attribution of sex through language are thus an interest
of mankind, and the genitals of speech are, as it were, the
means of its propagation. But what, if some higher genius
had brought it down from the stars? How would that be?
Was this genius from among the stars involved on our
earth under the moon in such passions of love and weakness, of hate and fear that he entwined everything in
affection and hate, that he imbued all words with fear and
joy, that in fine he built everything on acts of copulation?
Did he so see and feel as a man sees and feels that the
nouns, to him, had to join in the sex and gender, that he
brought together the verbs in action and suffering, that he
ascribed to them so many true and promiscuous children,
in short, that he built all of language on the feeling of
human weaknesses? Did he thus see and feel?

To an upholder of the supernatural origin of language
it is a matter of divine order "that most stem words are
monosyllabic, that the verbs are mostly bisyllabic, and
that language is thus divided according to criteria of

memory."[3] The fact is not accurate and the conclusion is uncertain. In the remains of the language considered to be the oldest, the roots are all bisyllabic verbs, a fact I can well explain on the basis of the foregoing, while the opposite hypothesis finds no reason for it. Those verbs are built directly on the tones and interjections of sounding nature. They often continue to echo in them, and here and there they are preserved as interjections. Mostly, to be sure, being half-inarticulate sounds, they were bound to be lost as the formation of language progressed. The first attempts of the stammering tongue are thus lacking in the Oriental languages, but the very fact that they are lacking and that only their regularized remnants echo in the verbs, bears witness to the originality and—humanity of language. Are these stems treasures and abstractions from the reason of God, or are they the first sounds of the listening ear, the first tones of the stammering tongue? The human race in its childhood formed language for itself precisely as it is stammered by the immature: it is the babbling vocabulary of the nursery. Where does it survive in the mouth of the adult?

What was said by so many of the Ancients, what in modern times has so often been repeated without understanding, derives from this its living reality: "That poetry is older than prose!" For what was this first language of ours other than a collection of elements of poetry? Imitation it was of sounding, acting, stirring nature! Taken from the interjections of all beings and animated by the interjections of human emotion! The natural language of all beings fashioned by reason into sounds, into images of action, passion, and living impact! A dictionary of the soul that was simultaneously mythology and a marvelous epic of the actions and the speech of all beings! Thus a contin-

---

[3] Süssmilch, §8 [actually, §7, note].

uous fabulation with passion and interest!—What else is
poetry?

And then: The tradition of Antiquity says that the first
language of the human race was song, and many good
musical people have hence imagined that man may well
have learned that song from the birds.—That indeed is
imagining a great deal! A great ponderous clock with all
its sharp wheels and newly tensed springs and hundred-
pound weights can well produce a carillon of tones; but
to put down newly created man with his active main-
springs, with his needs, with his strong emotions, with
his almost blindly preoccupied attention, and finally with
his brute throat, and to have him ape the nightingale and
derive language from singing after it—no matter how
many histories of music and poetry say so—is more than I
can understand. To be sure, a language through musical
tones would be possible—as Leibnitz,[4] too, has thought of
it—but for our earliest forebears, still in the state of
nature, this language was not possible. It is too artful and
refined. In the procession of beings each has its own
voice and a language after its own voice. The language
of love in the nest of the nightingale is sweet song; in the
cave of the lion it is a roar; in the forest it is the troating
of the buck deer and in the hiding place of cats a cater-
waul. Every species speaks its own language of love, not
for man, but for itself, a language as pleasant to itself as
was Petrarch's song to his Laura. As little, then, as the
nightingale sings—as some imagine—to entertain man,
so little can man ever be minded to invent for himself a
language by trilling the trills of the nightingale. And what
a monstrosity: A human nightingale in a cave or out in
the forest with the hunt!

If then the first language of man was song, it was song

---

[4] *Oeuvres philosophiques,* publiées p. Raspe [*Philosophical Works,*
ed. Raspe], p. 232.

as natural to him, as commensurate with his organs and his natural drives as the nightingale's song is to the nightingale which is, as it were, a winged lung; and that was —that was precisely our sounding language. Here, Condillac, Rousseau, and others did halfway find the road in that they derived the prosody and the song of the oldest languages from outcries of emotion, and there can be no doubt that emotion did indeed animate and elevate the first tones. But as mere tones of emotion could never be the origin of human language (which, after all, was what this song was), something is still wanting to produce it, and that, once again, was the naming of every creature after its own language. There then all of nature sang and sounded its recital, and the song of man was a concert of all those voices as far as his reason had use for them, as far as his emotions grasped them, as far as his organs could express them.—It was song, but it was neither the song of the nightingale nor the musical language of Leibnitz, nor a mere screaming of animal emotion. It was an expression of the language of all creatures within the natural scale of the human voice!

Even when subsequently language became more regular, more unisonant, and more orderly, it still remained a kind of song, as the accents of so many savages attest. And that this song—eventually sublimated and refined —gave rise to the oldest poetry and music, has by now been proven by more than one. The philosophical Englishman,[5] who in our century took up this matter of the origin of poetry and music, would have been able to progress farthest if he had not excluded the spirit of language from his investigation and if, instead of concerning himself so much with his system of bringing poetry and music to a single focus (in which neither

[5] Brown.

can show itself properly), he had concerned himself more with the origin of both from the full nature of man. In any event, since the best samples of the poetry of the Ancients are remnants from the times of the sung language, there are bound to be innumerable instances of misapprehension, of falsifications, and of misalignment and bad taste spelled out from the continuity of the oldest poems, of the tragedies of the Greeks, and of their declamation. How much remains to be said on this point for a philosopher who has learned, among the savages amongst whom that age is still alive, the right tone for reading those pieces! Otherwise and commonly one sees nothing but the texture of the wrong side of a tapestry! *Disiecti membra poetae!*—But I might go endlessly afield if I were to allow myself to make individual linguistic comments. So back to the high road of the invention of language!

How tones, when fashioned by reason into characteristic marks, would turn into words was easily understood; but not all objects sound. Whence now take for these objects characteristic words by which the soul might name them? Whence comes to man the art of changing into sound what is not sound? What has a color, what has roundness in common with the name that might evolve from it as the name bleating evolves from the sheep?—The protagonists of the supernatural origin of language have their answer ready-made: "Arbitrary! Who can understand and search God's reason for why green is called green and not blue? He no doubt wanted it that way!" And that cuts the argument short! All philosophizing about the skilled invention of language is thus arbitrarily suspended in the clouds, and for us every word is an occult quality, an arbitrary decision!—I trust no one will blame me if in this case I cannot understand the meaning of the word arbitrary. To invent a language out of one's brain, arbitrarily and without any basis of choice, is—at least for a human soul that wants to have a reason, some reason for everything—no less of a torture than it is for the body to be caressed to death. And then, we are here concerned with a sensuous, unrefined human being in the state of nature, whose forces have not as yet been sufficiently sublimated for him to play along purposelessly, who—strong and inexperienced—will do nothing without an urgent cause and nothing in vain. With him the invention of language in idle, vacuous arbitrariness runs quite contrary to every analogy of his nature. An arbitrarily thought-out language is in all senses contrary to the entire analogy of man's spiritual forces.

And so back to our subject. How could man, left to his own devices, invent

II. A *Language where No Sound Sounded for Him?*

What is the interconnection of vision and hearing, of color and word, of fragrance and sound?

Not among themselves in the objects. But what are these properties in the objects? They are no more than sense perceptions within us, and as such do they not all commingle into one? We are a single thinking *sensorium commune,* touched from various sides. There lies the explanation.

At the basis of all the senses there is sensation, and this established for the most varied forms of sensation so intimate, so strong, so ineffable a bond that from this interconnection the strangest phenomena arise. I know of more than one instance where an individual—naturally and possibly under the impression of something retained from childhood—could not but associate, by a direct and rapid impulse, this particular sound with that particular color, this particular phenomenon with that particular dark and quite different feeling, where a comparison through slow reason could detect no relationship whatever. For who can compare sound and color or phenomenon and feeling? We are full of such interconnections of the most different senses. We just do not notice them except under the impact of impulses which make us lose our composure, in morbid conditions of our imagination, or on occasions when they become exceptionally noticeable. The normal course of our thought is so fast, the waves of our emotions commingle so darkly: there is all at once so much in our soul that, with respect to most ideas, we are as though slumbering by a brook where to be sure we still hear the rushing of every wave, but so darkly that in the end sleep takes away from us all noticeable feeling. If it were possible for us to stop the moving chain of our thoughts to search each link for its connections—what strange discoveries there would be! What remarkable analogies of the most diverse senses according to which nonetheless the soul acts as a matter of course! We would all be, for a being endowed exclusively with reason, quite similar to the species of mental patients who think intelligently but associate most incomprehensibly and irrationally.

With sensuous beings, who perceive through many diverse senses at once, such an assembly of ideas is inevitable, for what else are all the senses but forms of perception of a single positive force of the soul? We distinguish them, but again only through our senses: that is, forms of perception through forms of perception. We learn by dint of great effort to differentiate them in the use we make of them, but at a certain depth they still continue to work together. All the analyses of sensation assumed by Buffon, Condillac, and Bonnet in feeling-endowed man are abstractions. The philosopher must abandon one thread of feeling as he pursues another. But in nature all the threads are one single tissue. The

darker the senses, the more they commingle; the greater
a man's lack of experience, that is, the less he is trained
to use one without another, to use it with skill and
clearly, the greater the darkness!—Let us apply this to
the beginning of language. The childhood and inexperience of the human race made it easier!

Man entered the world: What ocean rushed in on him
all at once! With what effort did he learn to differentiate!
to recognize his senses! to use individually the senses
thus recognized! The sense of vision is the coldest sense,
and if it had always been so cold, so remote, so clear
as for us it has come to be, through the effort and exercise
of many years, to be sure, I do not see how one could
make audible what one sees. However, nature took its
precautions and drew the distance closer: for in the beginning this sense of vision—as children and those previously blind can prove—was likewise no more than
feeling. Most visible things move. Many sound while
moving. If not, they lie close to the eye in its early state,
directly on it as it were and can be felt. The sense of
feeling is close to that of hearing. Its epithets—such as
hard, rough, soft, woolly, velvety, hairy, rigid, smooth,
prickly, etc., which all concern only surfaces and do not
penetrate—all sound as though one could feel them. The
soul, caught in the throng of such converging sensations
and needing to create a word, reached out and grasped
possibly the word of an adjacent sense whose feeling
flowed together with the first. Thus words arose for all
senses, including the coldest. Lightning does not sound;
but if now it is to be expressed, this messenger of mid-
night darkness!

> Which in a moment now uncovers heaven and earth
> And ere a man finds time to say "Look there!"
> Went down already into gaping darkness—

Of course, a word will do it that gives the ear, with the
help of an intermediate sensation, the feeling of sud-
denness and rapidity which the eye had of lightning.
Words like smell, tone, sweet, bitter, sour, and so on,
all sound as one feels, for what, originally, are the senses
other than feeling?—And how feeling can manifest itself
in sound, that we already accepted in the first section
as an immediate law of nature to which a feeling mechanism is subject and which we are not in a position to
explain in greater detail!

And thus all difficulties are reduced to the following
two postulates which have clearly been demonstrated.

1. Since all senses are nothing but forms of perception of the soul: assume only that it have distinct perception and hence distinguishing marks—with the distinguishing marks it does have inner language.

2. Since all the senses, especially in the state of human childhood, are nothing but forms of feeling of one
soul, and since further—in accordance with a law of
sensation of animal nature—all feeling has its sound
directly, it is but necessary that this feeling be raised
to the clarity of a distinguishing mark, and the word for
the external language is there. Here we touch upon numerous remarkable observations regarding nature's wisdom in organizing man for the task of inventing language
for himself. The principal point is this:

"Since man receives the language of teaching nature
only through the sense of hearing and could not invent
language without it, hearing has in a certain sense come
to be the middle one of his senses, the gateway to his
soul, and the connecting link among the remaining
senses." I shall explain.

1. Hearing is the middle one of the human senses in
its range of receptivity from outside. The sense of touch

senses only within itself and within its organ, while vision casts us by great distances outside of ourselves. Hearing stands in between in its degree of communicability. What that means for language? Assume a creature —even a rational creature—to whom the sense of touch would be (if it were possible) the major sense. How narrow is its world! And since it cannot perceive this world through the sense of hearing, it may possibly— without sounds—build for itself a language as an insect builds a web. Now assume a creature, all eye—how inexhaustible is the world of its beholdings! How immeasurably far is it cast outside itself! In what infinite multiplicity is it dispersed! Its language—we cannot form an idea of it—would be a kind of infinitely refined pantomime; its script an algebra built on colors and strokes —but sounding language, never! We creatures of hearing stand in the middle: We see, we feel; but the nature we see, the nature we feel, sounds! It teaches us language through sounds! We turn, as it were, into hearing through all our senses!

Let us appreciate the convenience of our position— through it every sense becomes language-apt. To be sure, only hearing really yields sounds, and man can invent nothing, can only find and emulate. But on the one side the sense of touch lies close by and on the other vision is the adjacent sense. The sensations unite and all converge in the area where distinguishing traits turn into sounds. Thus, what man sees with his eye and feels by touch can also become soundable. The sense for language has become our central and unifying sense; we are creatures of language.

2. Hearing is the middle one among the senses in distinctness and clarity and thus once again the sense for language. How vague is the sense of touch! It can be

overridden! It perceives all things merged. It would be difficult to sort out a characteristic mark for recognition: it would not be utterable!

Again, the sense of vision is so bright and overly brilliant, it supplies such a wealth of characteristic marks that the soul appears crushed under their multiplicity and can sort out one from among them only so weakly that recognition by it becomes difficult. The sense of hearing is in the middle. All the darkly commingled characteristic marks of the sense of touch it lets lie and so, too, the excessively fine characteristic marks of the sense of vision. But now there erupts from the touched and seen object a sound. Into it are gathered the characteristic marks of the other two senses, and it becomes the distinguishing word! Hearing thus reaches out and takes in on both sides: makes clear the excessively dark and more pleasing the excessively bright; carries into the dark many-sidedness of touch more unity and into the excessively bright many-sidedness of vision likewise. And as this recognition of many-sidedness turns, by means of one thing, by means of one characteristic mark, into language, it is the organ of language.

3. Hearing is the middle sense with respect to its vividness and hence is the sense of language. Touch overwhelms; vision is too cold and aloof. The former cuts into us too deeply to be qualified for becoming language; the latter remains too quiet before us. The tone of the sense of hearing goes into our soul so intimately that it must become a distinguishing mark, yet not so overpoweringly that, as a distinguishing mark, it loses its clarity—it is the sense of language.

How short, how tiring and unbearable would be the language of any coarser sense for us! How confusing and mind-voiding the language of the excessively refined sense of vision! Who could forever taste, touch, and smell without soon dying—as Pope has it—an aromatic death? And who could forever gape attentively at a color organ without soon going blind? But the experience of hearing—of thinking words, as it were, while hearing—is one we can endure longer and at almost any time. Hearing is to the soul what the green, the intermediate color is to the sense of vision. Man is organized to be a creature of language.

4. Hearing is the middle sense with respect to the time interval of its effect and hence is the sense of language. The sense of touch throws all things into us at once: it strongly plucks the chords but does so briefly and abruptly. The sense of vision presents to us all things at once and frightens the apprentice by its boundless array of juxtaposed displays. Through the sense of hearing, note how gently our teacher of language deals with us! It counts out the tones and pours them into the soul one at a time, it keeps giving and does not tire, keeps giving and has forever more to give. It practices the art of method: it teaches progressively! Who could not thus grasp language? Invent language?

5. The sense of hearing is the middle sense in regard to the needs of expression and is hence the sense of language. The impression of the sense of touch is ineffably dark; the less therefore can it be uttered. It is of such direct concern to us! It is so centered and so submerged in itself!—The impression of the sense of vision is unutterable for the inventor of language. But then what need is there to utter at once? The objects remain. They can be shown by gestures. The objects of hearing, however, are associated with movement. They pass by, and through that, they sound. They become utterable because they must be uttered, and through the need to be uttered, through their movement, they become utterable. —What qualification for language!

6. The sense of hearing is the middle sense in regard
to its development and thus the sense of language. Man
is tactile feeling in his entirety: The embryo, in the first
moment of life, feels as the newborn does. That is the
trunk of nature from which sprout the more delicate
branches of sensuousness, the wound-up ball of yarn
from which unroll all the finer forces of the soul. How
do they do this? As we have seen, through the sense of
hearing, for it is through sounds that nature awakens the
soul to a first distinct sensation, awakens it, as it were,
from the dark sleep of tactile feeling to have it mature
to a still finer sensuousness. If, for example, the sense of
vision were developed before it or if it were possible
that it be awakened from tactile feeling by means other
than the intermediate sense of hearing—what poverty
in wisdom! What stupidity in clairvoyance! How difficult would it be for such an all-eyed creature, if it were
still to be human, to name what it sees, to bind into one
the coldness of vision with the warmth of touch, with
the entire continuity of mankind. But the assumption
itself is contradictory: The road of human development
which nature has chosen is better and is unique. Since all
the senses work together, we are, through the sense of
hearing, at all times, so to speak, in the school of nature,
learning how to abstract, and simultaneously how to
speak. The sense of vision is refined with reason: reason
with the gift of naming. And thus, as man achieves the
finest characterization of visible phenomena—what a
treasury of language and of language similitudes lies
ready for use. He took the road from feelings of touch
into the sense of his imaginings via the sense of language and learned thus to sound what he perceives by
vision as well as what he perceives by touch.

If now at this point I could gather up all the loose
ends and make at once visible the woven texture called

human nature—in all its parts a texture for language! For that, we have seen, space and sphere were assigned to this positive power of thought: for that its substance and its matter were meted out; for that its shape and its form were created; for that its senses organized and aligned—for language! That is why man thinks neither more brightly nor more darkly; why he sees not and feels not more keenly, more lastingly, more vividly; why he has these and not more and not other senses. All things are balanced against one another. In economy and substitution! Laid out and distributed with a purpose! Unity and coherence! Proportion and order! A whole! A system! A creature of reflection and language, of the power to reflect and to create language! If anyone, after all these observations, were still ready to deny man's being destined to be a creature of language, he first would have to turn from being an observer of nature into being its destroyer! Would have to break into dissonance all the harmonies shown; lay waste the whole splendid structure of human forces, corrupt his sensuousness, and sense instead of nature's masterpiece a creature full of wants and lacunae, full of weaknesses and convulsions! And if now, on the other hand, language is precisely as it arose of necessity and in accordance with the plan and the might of the creature described?

I shall proceed to prove this last point, although I might take this occasion for a most pleasant excursus and calculate according to the rules of Sulzer's theory of pleasure what advantages and conveniences a language through the sense of hearing has for us in comparison with the language of the other senses.—But the excursus would take me too far afield and I must forsake it, while the main road still needs to be secured and rectified.—So then firstly

I. "The older and the more original languages are,

the more is this analogy of the senses noticeable in their roots."

Where with later languages we characterize wrath in its roots as a phenomenon of the face or as an abstract concept—for instance through the sparkle of the eyes or a glowing of the cheeks and the like—and hence merely see or think it, the Oriental hears it, hears it roar, hears it burst out in burning smoke and storming sparks! That became the stem of the word: the nostrils the seat of wrath; the whole family of words and metaphors of wrath snort out their origin.

If to us life manifests itself through the pulse beat, through surging blood and delicate marks of characterization also in language, to him it revealed itself through audible breathing. Man lived while he respired; he died as he expired. And the root of the word could be heard as the first animated Adam was heard to respire.

While we characterize child-bearing in our way, he again hears in the corresponding designations the screams of the frightened mother or again in animals the emptying of the amniotic sac. All his images revolve about this central idea.

Where in the word dawn we faintly hear an element of beauty, brilliance, and freshness, a lingering wanderer in the Orient feels in the very root of the word the first quick delightful ray of light which the like of us has never seen or at least has never felt with full feeling.— Examples from old and unsophisticated languages, showing how warmly and with what strong emotion they characterize from hearing and feeling, are numberless. And a work of the kind that would thoroughly trace the basic feeling of such ideas in various peoples, would be a full demonstration of my postulate and of the human invention of language.

II. "The older and the more original languages are,

the more the feelings intertwine in the roots of the words!"

Open at random an Oriental dictionary, and you will see the urge to express! How these inventors tore ideas away from one feeling to use them in the expression of another! How they did this borrowing most extensively from the heaviest, coldest, keenest senses! How everything had to turn into feeling and sound before it could turn into expression! Hence those powerful bold metaphors in the roots of the words! Hence the transpositions from feeling to feeling until the significations of a stem word, and still more of its branches seen side by side, form a most colorful, motley array. The genetic cause of this lies in the poverty of the human soul and in the convergence of all sensations in the unrefined individual. We see clearly his need to express himself: We see it the more, the more remote the idea was from the feeling and the tone of sensation, so that it is no longer possible to doubt the human origin of language. For how would the protagonists of another genesis explain this intertwining of ideas in the roots of the words? Was God so lacking in ideas and words that he had to have recourse to that kind of confusing word usage? Or was he so enamored of hyperbole, of far-fetched metaphors that he impressed this spirit upon the very roots of his language?

The so-called language of God, Hebrew, is totally imbued with such boldnesses, and rightly does the Orient claim the honor of designating it with its name. But beware of calling this spirit of metaphors Asian, as though it were not to be found anywhere else! It is alive in all unpolished languages, though, to be sure, according to the degree of each nation's culture and the specific character of its way of thinking. A people not wont to subject its feelings to thorough and keen differentiation, a people not endowed with the ardor to express itself and to take hold with sovereign unconcern of expressions wherever they might be found—such a people will not worry much about fine shades of feeling and will make do with slow-paced half-expressions. A fiery people reveals its boldness in its metaphors, whether it inhabits the Orient or North America. But where in the deepest depths such transplantations are to be found in the greatest numbers, there the language was by far the least endowed, was the oldest and most original, and that—without doubt—takes us to the Orient.

It is apparent what a difficult undertaking a true etymological survey would be in such a language. Those varied significations of one root that are to be traced and reduced to their origin in its genealogical tree are interrelated by no more than vague feelings, transient side associations, and perceptional echoes which arise from the depth of the soul and can hardly be covered by rules. Furthermore, their interrelations are so specifically national, so much in conformity with the manner of thinking and seeing of the people, of the inventor, in a particular country, in a particular time, under particular circumstances, that it is exceedingly difficult for a Northerner and Westerner to strike them right and that they must suffer greatly in long-winded and cold-hearted circumlocutions. And since they were demanded by necessity and invented in a state of feeling and arousal to satisfy an expressive want—what rare good luck would not be needed to strike the very same note? And since finally in a dictionary of this kind the words and the significations of a word are to be gathered from such diverse times, occasions, and ways of thinking, and since thus these momentary determinations appear infinitely augmented—how then is not the difficulty multiplied! What keen insight is needed to penetrate into those circumstances and into those requirements and what moderation to avoid all excess in the interpretation of various times! How much knowledge, how much adaptability of mind is not needed to acquire fully the native wit, the bold imagination, the national feelings of such remote ages, and to modernize them in accordance with ours! Yet the venture would not simply elucidate the history, the forms of thought, and the literature of a particular country, it would quite universally carry a torch to the dark recesses of the human soul where concepts commingle and intertwine, where the most diverse feelings engender one another, where an urgent occasion musters all forces of the soul, revealing the whole range of inventive powers with which it is endowed. Every step in that endeavor would mark a discovery and every new observation would represent the most complete proof of the human origin of language.

Schultens has the great merit of having elaborated a number of such origins in the Hebrew language. And each of his elaborations provides proof of my thesis. But for a variety of reasons, I do not believe that the origins of the first human language, even though it were Hebrew, can ever be completely elaborated.

I must still argue out a note which is too general and too important to be omitted. The basis and the cause of such bold verbal metaphors lay in their original invention. But what when much later, with the need long since satisfied, such species of words and of imagery survive or, indeed, are extended and increased in sheer imitation or for the love of things past? Then, oh yes, then the product turns out to be sublime nonsense, a turgid play with words which, in the beginning, it most certainly was not. In the beginning it was bold and virile acuity, which doubtless was the least intent upon playing where it seemed the most to play. It was unschooled sublimity of imagination that worked out such feelings in such words. But now, as used by stale imitators without such feeling and without such occasion, alas, they are vials of words which the spirit has left; and that, in later times, has been the fate of all the languages in which the first forms were so bold. French writers of later times cannot lose themselves in the clouds because the first inventors of their language did not lose themselves in the clouds. Their entire language is prose of sound reason and has, by origin, almost no poetic word, almost none that would be peculiar to the poet. But the Orientals? The Greeks? The British? And we Germans?

From this it follows that, the older a language and the more such boldnesses in its roots—if it has lived a long time and has evolved a long time—the less is it permissible to jump at every original boldness as though each one of all those mutually intertwined concepts were always consciously present in every later application. The metaphor of the beginning was the urge to speak. If later, when the word is current and its keenness blunted, the combination of such disparities is regarded as proof of fertility and energy—what miserable specimens are not then spawned in whole schools in the Oriental languages!

And one more thing. If now such bold verbal labors, such transpositions of feelings into a term, such ruleless and lineless meshings of ideas appear as the basis, or are made to be the basis, on which the refined concepts of a dogma or a system are to be tacked or in which such concepts are to be studied—heavens! how little were these verbal trials of a nascent or immature language definitions of a system and how often is one led to create word idols of which the inventor and subsequent usage knew nothing!—But such comments could go on forever. I proceed with another canon.

III. "The more original a language and the more fre-

quently such feelings appear intertwined in it, the less
is it possible for them to be subordinated to one another
with precision and logic. Language is rich in synonyms.
With all its inadequacies in essentials, it has the greatest
unnecessary abundance."

The upholders of the divine origin, who manage to
discover divine order in everything, are hard put to it
to find it here, and they deny that there are synonyms.[6]
They deny? Well now, let it be assumed that among the
fifty words which the Arabs have for the lion, among
the two hundred which they have for the snake, or the
eighty for honey and the more than a thousand which
they have for the sword, nice differences can be found,
that is, were once present and have since vanished—
why if they had to vanish were they present? Why did
God invent an unnecessary wealth of words which, as
the Arabs claim, only a divine prophet could grasp in
its entire range? Was he inventing into a vacuum of
oblivion? Relatively speaking, these words are still synonyms, considering the numerous other ideas for which
words are totally missing. Now trace, if you can, divine
order in the fact that a god, who saw the plan of language as a whole, invented seventy words for the stone
and none for all the indispensable ideas, innermost feelings, and abstractions, that in one case he drowned us
in unnecessary abundance while leaving us in the other
in the direst need which obliged us to steal and usurp
metaphors and talk half nonsense, etc.

In human terms the thing is easily explained. While
difficult and rare ideas had to be expressed indirectly,
those that were at hand and easy could find frequent
expression. The more unfamiliar man was with nature,
that is, the more numerous the angles under which in

---

[6] Süssmilch, §9.

his inexperience he looked at it, hardly able to recognize it again, and the less he invented *a priori* but instead in accordance with sensuous circumstances, the more synonyms had to arise! The more numerous the individuals who did the inventing and the more they did so roaming by themselves and in isolation, inventing in general terms only within their own circle for identical things; when later on they foregathered, when their languages streamed out into an ocean of vocabulary, the more synonyms there were. None could be rejected, for which should have been? They were in use with this tribe, this clan, this singer. And so, as the Arab compiler of a dictionary put it when he had enumerated four hundred words for misery, it was a four hundred first misery to be obliged to list the words for misery. Such a language is rich because it is poor, because its inventors did not have plan enough to grow poor. And we are to believe that the idle inventor of such an outstandingly imperfect language was God?

The analogies of all languages still in the state of nature confirm my thesis: Each in its own way is both lavish and lacking, but, to be sure, each in its own way. If the Arabs have so many words for stone, camel, sword, snake (things amongst which they live), the language of Ceylon, in accordance with the inclination of its people, is rich in flatteries, titles, and verbal décor. For the term "woman" it has, according to rank and class, twelve different names, while we discourteous Germans, for example, are forced in this to borrow from our neighbors. According to class, rank, and number, you is rendered in sixteen different ways, and this as well in the language of the journeyman as in that of the courtier. Profusion is the style of the language. In Siam there are eight different ways of saying I and we, depending on whether the master speaks to the servant or the servant

to the master. The language of the savage Caribs is
virtually divided in two, one for women and one for
men, and the most common objects—bed, moon, sun,
bow—are named differently in the two. What a super-
fluity of synonyms! And yet these same Caribs have only
four words for colors, to which they must refer all others.
What paucity!—The Hurons have consistently double
verbs for animate and inanimate things, so that to see,
when it is "to see a stone" and to see, when it is "to see
a man" are two different terms. Pursue this through all
of nature. What wealth! To make use of a thing one owns
or to make use of a thing owned by him to whom one is
speaking is always expressed by two different words.
What wealth!—In the main language of Peru, blood
relations are termed in such remarkable segmentation
that the sister of the brother and the sister of the sister,
the child of the father and the child of the mother have
quite different designations, and yet this same language
has not really a plural.—Each one of these synonymies
is linked to custom, character, and origin of the people;
and everywhere the inventive human spirit reveals itself.
—Still another canon:

IV. "As the human soul can recall no abstraction from
the realm of the spirits to which it did not advance
through opportunities and arousals of the senses, so no
language has an abstract term to which it was not led
through tone and feeling. And the more original a language, the fewer its abstractions and the more numerous
its feelings." Once again, I can in this limitless field do
no more than gather flowers:

The entire structure of the Oriental languages bears
witness to the fact that all their abstracts were once
sensates. Spirit was wind, breath, nocturnal storm. Sacred was called set-off, solitudinous. The soul was called
breathing, wrath the snorting of the nose, etc. The more

general concepts were thus evolved in them only later on through abstraction, perception, fantasy, simile, analogy, etc.—None lies in the deepest depths of language.

Among all savages the same holds true according to their level of culture. In the language of Barantola no word for sacred and among the Hottentots no word for spirit could be found. All missionaries throughout the world complain about the difficulty of communicating Christian concepts to the natives, in the language of the natives; and yet such communications are doubtless not concerned with scholastic dogma but only with common concepts of common reason. As one reads here and there translated specimens of versions made for natives or even for speakers of the unpolished languages of Europe—such as the languages of the Lapps, the Finns, the Esthonians—and compares the grammars and dictionaries of such peoples, the difficulties are plain to see.

And if one prefers not to believe the missionaries, then one can read the philosophers, de la Condamine in Peru and along the Amazon, Maupertuis in Lapland, etc. Time, duration, space, essence, substance, body, virtue, justice, freedom, appreciation are not to be heard from the mouths of the Peruvians, even though they show by their manner of reasoning that they conclude according to such concepts and by their actions that they possess such virtues. As long as an idea has not become clear to them, has not been used by them as a distinguishing mark, they have no corresponding word.

Wherever such words have entered the language, they clearly show their origin. The Church language of the Russian nation is primarily Greek. The Christian concepts of the Letts are German words or German concepts Lettified. The Mexican wishing to express his idea of a poor sinner depicts him as a person kneeling in auricular confession and his trinity as three faces with halos. We all know by what pathways most abstractions came into our languages of science, of theology and jurisprudence, of philosophy and the like. We all know how often scholasticists and polemicists were unable to carry out their fights with words of their own language and therefore had to go and borrow their weapons (hypostasis and substance, homoousios and homoiousios) from those languages in which the concepts had been abstracted, in which the weapons had been tempered! Our entire psychology, however refined and defined it may be, has not a single word of its own.

This is so true that even the illuminati in their frenzy do not find it possible to characterize their new secrets from nature or heaven and hell by means other than imagery and sensuous conceptions. Swedenborg, in piecing together his angels and spirits, could not but use snippets from all the senses, and the sublime Klopstock, the greatest antithesis of the former, could not but build his heaven and hell from sensuous materials. The Negro scents the presence of his gods from the treetops, the Chinghailese finds his devil by hearing him in the rustling of the forests. I have stalked some of these abstractions in various languages among various peoples and have found the most remarkable inventive tricks of the human mind. The subject is much too vast. The base, however, is always the same. When the savage surmises that this particular thing has a spirit, then a particular sensuous thing must exist from which he can abstract that spirit. Though, to be sure, abstraction has diverse varieties, stages, and methods. The simplest example to show that no nation has in its language more words and words other than it has learned to abstract is to be seen in the no doubt easy abstraction of the numerals. How few do most savages possess, no matter how rich, how excellent, and elaborate their languages may be. Never more than

their needs call for. The trading Phoenican was the first
to invent the art of numeration. The herdsman checking
his herd learns naturally how to count. Nations of hunters,
never involved in concerns of multiple numbers, know
how to describe an army only as being like the hair on
the head. Who can count hair? Who, without ever having
counted that far, has words to do so?

Is it possible to look away from all these traces of the
roaming, language-making spirit, and to seek the origin
of language in the clouds? What proof is there of the
existence of a single word which only God could invent?
Is there in any language anywhere a single, pure and
universal concept that was handed down to man from
Heaven? Where is even the possibility for such a concept? [7]—But a hundred thousand reasons and analogies
and proofs of the genesis of language in the human soul,
in accordance with human senses, human ways of perception! Proofs of the advance of language with reason,
of its development from reason among all peoples, in all
zones, under all conditions! What ear can fail to hear
this universal voice of nations?

And yet I see with amazement that once again Herr
Süssmilch comes to meet me, discovering divine order
where I see the most human. [8] "That so far no language
has been discovered that was totally unfit for the arts
and the sciences," what else does this prove but that no
language is bestial and that all languages are human?
Where has a human being been found quite unfit for the
arts and the sciences? And was that cause for wonder or
was it the most ordinary thing because he was a human

[7] The best treatise I have seen on this subject is by an Englishman:
*Things divine & supernatural conceived by analogy with things nat-
ural and human,* London, 1755, by the author of *the procedure,
extent and limits of human understanding.*
[8] Süssmilch, §11.

being? "All missionaries have been able to talk to the most savage peoples and have been able to convince them. That could not be done without conclusions and without arguments. Hence their languages had to contain abstract terms, etc." And if so, was it divine order? Or was it not simply a most human thing to produce terms by abstraction where they were needed? And what people has ever had a single abstraction in its language that was not acquired by that people itself? And were there equal numbers of them for all peoples? Did missionaries find it everywhere equally easy to express themselves or have we not read the opposite from all parts of the world? And how did they express themselves other than by molding their new concepts by analogy to the contours of the language before them? And was this done everywhere in the same way?—Much, very much could be said about the fact as such! The conclusion states the very opposite of what it has been made out to be. Precisely because human reason cannot be without abstraction and because no abstraction can be performed without language, it follows that in every people language must of necessity contain abstractions, that is, must of necessity be a copy of the power of reason by which it was used as a tool. But as each language contains only as many abstractions as its speakers were able to make and none that was made without senses (as is apparent from their originally sensuous expression), divine order is nowhere to be seen, except—except in so far as language in all its aspects is human.

V. Finally: "Since every grammar is only a philosophy of language and a method for its use, it follows that, the more primordial a language is, the less grammar must there be in it, and the oldest language is no more than the aforementioned dictionary of nature." I outline a few striking illustrations.

1. Declensions and conjugations are merely shortcuts and identifications in the use of nouns and verbs according to number, tense, mode, and person. Therefore, the less refined a language is, the less regular is it in these determinations, reflecting at every turn the course of human reason. In fine, without the art of usage, it is a simple dictionary.

2. As the verbs of a language are earlier than the nouns roundly abstracted from them, so also were there originally the more conjugations the less numerous the concepts one had learned to place in subordination to one another. How numerous are those the Orientals have! And yet there are really none, for how numerous everywhere are not the transpositions and translocations of verbs from one conjugation to another! The thing is quite natural. Since nothing concerns man or, at least, since nothing affects him in terms of language as deeply as what he is about to relate, deeds and acts and events, there must be gathered together, in the beginning, such a mass of deeds and events that a new verb arises for almost every state. "In the language of the Hurons everything is conjugated. An art which cannot be explained permits in it the distinction of verbs, nouns, pronouns, and adjectives. The simple verbs have a double conjugation, one for themselves and one relating to other things. The third persons have forms for the two sexes. As for the tenses, the same nice distinctions exist that are to be noted for instance in Greek. Indeed, in relating a journey, the expression differs depending on whether it was by land or by water. The active forms are multiplied as often as there are things to be covered by the doing. The term for to eat changes from one edible substance to another. Acts performed by an animate being are expressed differently from those done by an inanimate thing. Making use of one's own property and of that of

the person with whom one speaks has two forms of expression, etc."

Imagine this multiplicity of verbs, modes, tenses, persons, states, genders, etc.—What trouble and what art to keep all that somehow straightened out, to evolve somehow a grammar from what was no more than a vocabulary!—The grammar of Father Leri of the Topinambuans in Brazil shows just that.—For as the first vocabulary of the human soul was a living epic of sounding and acting nature, so the first grammar was almost nothing but a philosophical attempt to develop that epic into a more regularized history. Thus it works itself down with verbs and more verbs and keeps working in a chaos which is inexhaustible for poetry, which is very rich— when subjected to a little more order—for the fixing of history, and which becomes usable only much later for axioms and demonstrations.

3. The word which in imitation followed directly upon a sound of nature followed a thing that was past. Preterits are therefore the roots of verbs, but these are preterits which are still almost valid for the present. This fact must, *a priori*, seem strange and inexplicable, since the present time ought to be the first, as indeed it came to be in all languages of later development. According to the history of the invention of language it could not be otherwise. The present is something one shows; the past is something one must relate. And since it could be related in so many ways, and since—in the beginning, in the need to find words—it had to be done in many ways, there came into being, in all the old languages, many preterits but only one present or none at all. This then, in more civilized ages, was greatly to the advantage of poetry and history but very little to that of philosophy, for philosophy has no love of confusingly rich supplies. —Here again the Hurons, the Brazilians, the Orientals,

and the Greeks are alike: Everywhere traces of the development of the human mind.

4. All the more recent philosophical languages have modified the noun in greater refinement, the verb less so but more regularly, for these languages adapted themselves more and more to the needs of a detached contemplation of what is and in fact has been and ceased to be irregularly stammering mixtures of things that possibly were and perhaps persist. The habit arose to state one after the other the things that are and in fact have been and hence to define them through numbers and articles and cases, etc. The early inventors wanted to say everything at once, not just what appeared to have been done but also who did it and when and how and where it happened.[9] They thus carried into the noun the state; into every form of the verb the gender; they distinguished —by pre- and adformatives, by affixes and suffixes—the verb and the adverb, the verb and the noun, and all things flowed together. But later there came to be more and more differentiation, more and more enumerations: From breaths evolved articles, from starting clicks persons, from prestatements modes or adverbs. The parts of speech separated. Gradually grammar evolved. Thus the art of speech, this philosophy of language, evolved but slowly and gradually down through the centuries and ages, and the mind that was the first to think of a true philosophy of grammar, of "the art of speech," must of necessity have begun by thinking over, down through the generations and down its stages, its history. If only we had such a history! It would be, with all its deviations and excursuses, a charter of the humanity of language.

5. But how was it possible for a language to exist entirely without grammar? As a mere confluence of

---

[9] Rousseau divined this postulate in his hypothesis. I define and prove it.

images and sensations without coherence and definition?
—Both were cared for: It was a living language. In it
the great harmonizing power of gestures provided, as it
were, the order and sphere where things belonged; and
the great wealth of delimitations inherent in the vocabulary itself replaces the art of grammar. Consider the old
script of the Mexicans! They drew whole sequences of
individual pictures. And where no picture came to mind,
they agreed on strokes, and the coherence of it all must
be supplied by the world in which it belonged and from
which it was being divined. This art of divination, of
surmising coherence from detached signs, how far is it
not still being mastered by individual mute and deaf
persons! And if this art is an intrinsic part of the language, if it is learned, as language and with language,
from childhood up, if through tradition in the succession
of generations it becomes simplified and perfected, I
see in it nothing incomprehensible.—But then, the more
it becomes simplified, the more it declines; the more it
turns into grammar—and that is the stepwise progression
of the human mind.

Exemplifications of this are for instance the notes of
la Loubere on the language of Siam. How much it still
resembles the continuity of the Oriental languages, especially before a later development carried more structure into it. The Siamese who wants to say, "If I were in
Siam, I would be pleased," says in fact, "If I be city
Siam, I well heart much."—He wants to recite the Lord's
Prayer and must say, "Father, us be Heaven. Name God
want sacred all place, etc." How Oriental and how primordial! Quite as coherent as Mexican picture writing
or the stammering of the unsophisticated in a foreign
language.

6. There is still another peculiarity which I must explain here, and again one which I find to have been

misunderstood in Süssmilch's divine order, namely "the multiplicity of significations of a single word in accordance with the differentiation of minor aspects of articulation." I find this skill among almost all the savages; Garcilaso de la Vega, for instance, notes it for the Peruvians, Condamine for the Brazilians, la Loubere for the Siamese, Resnel for the North Americans. I find it likewise in the ancient languages, Chinese for instance, and the languages of the Orient, especially Hebrew, where a minor sound, accent, breath changes the whole meaning, and yet I find in this nothing I would not call very human, nothing but inadequacy and inertia of the inventors! They required a new word, and since leisurely invention from an empty head is difficult, they took a similar one with perhaps just a change of breath. This was a law of economy, quite natural to them with their pervading feelings, yet with their powerful enunciation of words, convenient. But for an outsider—whose ear is not accustomed to it from childhood on and who now gets something in that language hissed into his face, with half the sounds phlegmatically held back in the mouth—this law of economic expediency makes the language impossible to understand and to pronounce. The more a wholesome grammar makes for order in the household of a language, the less will such parsimony be necessary.—Hardly a hallmark of divine invention, that the inventor, for lack of ingenuity, had to fall back on such devices.

7. Most evident, finally, is the progress of language through reason and of reason through language when the latter has already taken some steps forward, when there are in it already works of art, such as poems, when a system of writing has been invented, when literary genres begin to evolve one after another. Then no step can be taken, no new word can be invented, no new

felicitous form can be put to use which does not carry
the imprint of the human soul. Then, through poetry,
come into being syllabic meter, choice of expressive words
and of colors, order and impact of imagery; then, through
history, come differentiation of tenses, precision of expression; then, through oratory, comes finally the perfect
rounding of periodic speech. If now, before the moment
of such an addition, nothing like it lay in the language
but was carried into it and could be carried into it by the
human soul, where then would one set limits to this pro-
ductivity, to this fertility? Where would one say: Here a
human soul began to act but not before? If it proved
able to invent the finest, the most difficult, why not the
easiest? If it was able to accomplish, why was it not able
to try, why not to begin? For what was the beginning
other than the production of one single word, as a sign
of reason? And this was for it an inescapable necessity,
however blind and mute it was within, as truly as it was
endowed with reason.

I believe that through the things I have said—pro-
ceeding, internally, from within the human soul and arguing, externally, on the basis of the organization of man
and by the analogy of all languages and all peoples,
partly in the component parts of all speech, partly with
respect to the grandiose overall progress of language in
correlation with reason—man's ability to invent language for himself has been demonstrated to such an
extent that no one can doubt it for one moment if he
does not deny man's reason or, which amounts to the
same thing, if he but knows what reason is, if, furthermore, he has ever concerned himself philosophically
with the elements of language and has, with the eyes
of an observer, considered the nature and the history
of the languages on earth. The genesis of language in

the human soul is as conclusively evident as any philosophical demonstration could be, and the external analogy of all ages, languages, and peoples imparts to it as high a degree of probability as is possible with the most certain events in history.

AFTERWORD

We think of Herder as the teacher of Goethe and the disciple of Hamann. If we are honest, we go on to admit that he is to us little more than a name we are wont to see in the histories of literature. The same holds true of his teacher. Not, however, of his disciple. There is tragedy in this, and a peculiar kind of greatness.

Herder was five years older than Goethe and fourteen years younger than Hamann. He was born in 1744 in Mohrungen in East Prussia, but he subsequently carried the heritage of nostalgic brooding of his native land south and west.

Hamann acquired the surname of "Magus of the North" and kept faith with it. His wisdom inspires momentary flashes of awe, but we learn to accept the impossibility of ever encompassing it in sustained comprehension.

Herder, in contrast to Hamann, went not only to live but also to compete in a world where classical clarity prevailed as the ultimate ideal. Having taught school for a number of years at Riga, he left the northeast for good at the age of twenty-five. In 1776 he gave up his post as pastor in Bückeburg, which he had held for five years, and became, on Goethe's recommendation, court chaplain and church superintendent in Weimar. He never quite outlived the last vestige of his bad conscience toward the oracular hermeticism of his teacher; and he never quite forgave Goethe for becoming a Goethe instead of a Herder. He held his posts in Weimar, which he owed to Goethe, to the time of his death in 1803.

When Herder and Goethe met for the first time in 1769 in Strasbourg, it was, as one historian of literature put it, as when water in a glass is immersed in water in a pail: a scarcely perceptible septum kept the two entities distinct. This bold and—in some of its implications— awkward image makes short shrift with all studies of the "influence" of Herder on Goethe. They are fascinating, as are all comparative studies (in literature as in anatomy), but when they seem to suggest that there is something in Goethe that would not have been there without Herder, they tread on very thin ice.

Something along these very same lines applies indeed to Herder's relation with all the leading protagonists of the ideas and principles we regard as characteristic of the turn of the eighteenth and the early part of the nineteenth centuries. It is quite evident that Herder was a precursor of the romantics, but again it is not only unnecessary but unrealistic to accuse any of them of having plagiarized him.

In any event, let the student of ideas—of the history of ideas—pick up any thread anywhere in the nineteenth century: if he pursues it back through the complex meshes of its past course, he will as rarely find it possible to bypass Herder as to bypass Goethe. Yet, there is a significant difference between the two situations. Tracing an idea to Goethe affords us the happy experience of an encounter with lucid formulations of keenly perceived views. In Herder we meet with allusions, must be content with the vague sensation of presences, have to learn to enjoy watching the turbid whirls of the processes of thinking in lieu of beholding the accomplished Gestalt of a thought.

Of all the ideas which determine and which characterize the course of nineteenth-century thought and its continuity into the present, none is more crucially vital than the idea of the organic entity and its organic growth. It pervades our historical thinking and determines our attitude toward all biological phenomena. We know it came to the fore in the age loosely referred to as the age of romanticism or—in German letters, specifically—as the age of Goethe. It illustrates beautifully, and symptomatically, the argument of the preceding passage, for no other concept is either more evidently or more ubiquitously alive in the thinking of both Goethe and Herder. In Goethe this concept led to the doctrine of the metamorphosis of plants and hence to the postulate of the reality "Plant," posited as an *ur*-phenomenon (with the prefix expressing both primordiality and sempiternity). In Herder, on the other hand. . . . But here it is unavoidable that we proceed somewhat more comprehensively.

First, it may be permitted to refer at this point, in seeming digression, to the diary which Herder kept in 1769 during his trip from Riga to Paris and thence to Strasbourg. The complete works of Herder (as published from 1827 to 1830) crowd sixty sizeable volumes, yet it is safe to assert that all Herder's major literary and philosophical preoccupations appear programmatically epitomized in his Journal of 1769. And in it we find numerous allusions to the problems of origin and growth: "The first word was life"; "Was North or South, Orient or Occident the *vagina hominum?*"; "What was the origin of the human race, of man's inventions, his arts, his religions?" In addition to such cryptic questions, there are in the Journal remarkably revealing self-appraisals: "Why must a first work always assume such gothic vastness in my hands?"; "For what reason am I destined to see only shadows and never to touch the reality of things?"

One cannot but feel that a monumentally annotated edition of the Journal might impart new life to many of the still viable portions of Herder's works. All the key passages in the essay on the origin of language would appear in the notes of such an edition, with lengthy excerpts—freed from all dross—from the *Ideas on the Philosophy of the History of Mankind* (on which Herder worked from 1784 to 1791) and from the *Letters for the Advancement of Humanity* (which were written between 1793 and 1797).

Second, we may insert (and utilize) at this point a quick reference to Herder's essay "On the Earliest Document of Mankind," which was published in 1774 (two years after the essay on the origin of language). The document regarded by Herder (and his contemporaries) as mankind's earliest was the first book of the Pentateuch, that is, Genesis.

In religious terms, Genesis describes the creation of the world. In philosophical, or—if you will (and Herder would)—in scientific terms, it describes the origin of the world. And here something unforgettable happens. Herder makes us read Genesis as a description of the awakening of day and life after the sleep and death of night. We find ourselves, before dawn, on a mountaintop while there is still darkness upon the face of the deep. The first event to occur is light, and it seems that a firmament is forced through the waters above and below, and on and on through all the familiar phases.

Thus guided by Herder, the modern reader experiences a renewed kind of poetic beauty in Genesis. This is as it should be. Herder will quite agree that there is beauty in it and that the beauty is poetic. But "poiesis" means "making," "producing," "creation," and to Herder the poetry of Genesis is scientific fact. Furthermore, the mystic claim of the identity of creation and dawn, of birth and growth, is to him a factual claim also.

Here now we have touched upon the fundamental dilemma in all of Herder's thought. Nothing can arise unless it exists; there can be no "origin" in an absolute sense. Yet, everything evolves, and if our probing thought pursues a line of evolution beyond its visible portion, it reaches—in going back—a point it must call the beginning.

At such junctures Goethe's classical sense of measure made him stop. From the German word for "origin," which is *Ursprung,* he took the prefix *"ur-"* and used it to suggest—even to assert—that, once it was combined with a given phenomenon, probing the origin of that phenomenon was as meaningless as to ask, "Who made God?" But Herder—once upon a time the teacher of Goethe, at all times the disciple of Hamann—probed on, had to probe on and speak on, overruling in torrents of aggressive dialectics his own awareness of the inadequacies in his argument.

Among man's "arts" and "inventions," with "origins" clamoring for such probing, none, it seems evident, could have carried greater appeal for a mind like Herder's than our faculty of speech. In 1769, the Berlin Academy of Science offered him the opportunity to gather together his scattered thoughts on the subject. It announced that the theme of its essay contest for 1770 (with January 1, 1771, as the closing date for the submission of entries) was to be: "Are men, left to their natural faculties, in a position to invent language, and by what means do they, by themselves, accomplish that invention?" As was customary in the eighteenth century the question was formulated in French; the entries, however, as was Herder's, could be written in German.

When the news of the Academy's proposal reached him, Herder was still in Riga. There is evidence that he had thought as early as 1764 (at the age of twenty) of composing an essay on the origin of language, writing, and grammar. In his *Fragments on Modern German Literature* (published in 1767) he had repeatedly referred to the problem. He was indeed ready for the Academy's proposal. In a letter to his publisher and friend, Hartknoch, written during the latter part of 1769 while he was in France, he characterized it as "an excellent, a great and truly philosophical question" and added, "quite as though meant for me."

The actual composition of the essay was not begun till sometime in December, 1770, during the last weeks of Herder's stay in Strasbourg. It was completed before Christmas and reached the Academy before the closing date. This incredible speed of composition accounts for some of the essay's stylistic flaws, but it also contributed to the fact that this work, more than any other by Herder, has the passionate honesty of an outburst of conviction and reflects none of the pedantic industry of a contestant's endeavor to win a prize. Yet the essay did win the prize and was published in 1772, in Berlin, "by order of the Academy of Science."

As submitted and initially published, the essay consisted of two parts. The subtitle of the first part was the question, "Could men, left to their natural abilities, invent language for themselves?" The second part had the subtitle, "In what way was man best able and in what way was it inescapable for him to invent language for himself?"

Our translation of Herder's prize essay is limited to the first part. It is quite apparent to the reader of the complete original that Herder wrote two parts for no reason other than that the question of the Academy consisted of two parts. In a summary at the end of Part One he stated explicitly that he considered his demonstration complete and added: "However, in order to abort forever all possible objections and in order to make the thesis—also outwardly, as it were—as certain as a philosophical truth can possibly be, let us now additionally proceed on the basis of all external circumstances and from the analogy of human nature to prove that it was inescapable for man to invent his language and to show under what conditions he was most suitably able to do so."

The advisability and indeed the necessity of omitting the second part of the essay from this translation seemed to impose itself in view of the fact that the central theme of Part Two is no longer the origin of language as such but the evolution of it in diverse forms. (The factual unsoundness of many of Herder's premises proves more obstructive in Part Two than it does in Part One, where the modern reader is rarely, if ever, prevented from following Herder's argument as a result of the fact that the twentieth century has more and sounder linguistic information than the eighteenth.)

A synoptic summary of the part here omitted can be presented in the form of the four "Laws of Nature" which are discussed in it and appear as the captions of its subdivisions. These "Laws of Nature" are:

1. "Man is a freely thinking and active being whose powers work on in progressive continuity, for which reason he is a creature of language."

2. "Man is by destiny a creature of the herd, that is, of society; and the continuous development of his language is hence natural, essential, and necessary to him."

3. "As it was impossible for the entire human race to remain one herd, so it also could not remain restricted to one language. There ensued the development of diverse national languages."

4. "As in all probab   the human race represents
one progressive whole oɪ one origin in one great economy, so likewise all languages and with them the chain
of all culture."

The modern reader of Herder's essay on the origin of
language is stopped—and doubly shocked—by its very
first sentence. He proceeds to read it again—and again—
but there can be no doubt: Herder does indeed say that
man, already as an animal, possesses language. For one
thing, the phrase, "as an animal," is teasingly unclear.
Is this a reference to man as an animal in the continuity
of evolution, or does it signify that man, as he is now, can
be viewed as an animal? Or should we remember the
lesson of Herder's presentation of Genesis and refuse to
try to differentiate between the two possible interpre-
tations? And secondly, we thought we had a right—did
we not?—to expect Herder to grasp the problem of the
origin of human speech more intrinsically and more comprehensively than is possible through a mere mechanical
derivation of it from the sounds of animals.

But it is good to be guided in the subsequent reading
of the entire essay by this double worry in unresolved
strength. After a few pages we do find some measure of
comfort in Herder's emphatic assertion that, while human
speech contains indeed elements that are clearly on the
level of animals sounds, these are disqualified, precisely
by reason of their perennial presence, for the role of
primordial stem forms from which all the components of
the complex whole evolved in a process of gradually increased sophistication. Human language—Herder avers,
thank God—differs in essence and not just in its evolutionary stage from animal sounds.

All this is taken by Herder to imply that he must base
his search for the origin of human language on an analysis of the more comprehensive problem of the difference

between man and animal. And with this he is drawn into a typically Herderian and hence somehow grandiose vicious circle. The difference between animal and man, analyzed by Herder in terms whose fascinating ingenuity remains impressive even to the doctrinaire of twentieth-century psychology, lies in something which—no matter whether you call it reason or (re)cognition or whatever— is the basis of man's ability to speak. In other words: the difference between man and animal is that man has human language; and he got his language because he was man and not animal; and before he was man, though this formulation would have struck Herder as meaningless, the first step toward the development of human language was either impossible (because the creature expected to be taking the step was an animal and hence incapable of it) or superfluous (because the creature assumed to be less than a man was in fact human and had already taken it).

There is no way out of the agony of this vicious circle, either within the framework of Herder's thought or—to wantonly interject at this point a boldly generalized assertion that is not really called for—on the basis of the most enlightened principles of twentieth-century thought. But there is, as it were, a bonus. Language, human language, of which speech is no more than the audible manifestation, is—to use Herder's phraseology—the faculty of the human soul to cognize and recognize or—to use modern terms—the power of the human mind to form concepts and to manipulate them in sovereign freedom and at a distance in time and in space from what they represent.

This is the essence of Herder's essay on the origin of language. It appears embedded in a mass of material of only historical interest, including many assertions of fact that make the proudly better-informed twentieth-century reader smile. But in the end we must ask: Can we today, armed as we are with an infinitely more vast array of documented primary data than Herder, excel over Herder in his ultimate insight into the nature and the mystery of language? The answer, I fear, can only be in the negative.

And so this "quaint" eighteenth-century essay—properly read—turns out, in its philosophical essence, to be timely and possibly timeless. In the course of the close of two centuries since the time of the original publication of Herder's essay on the origin of language, nothing has been said or written to replace or supersede its real substance (which is but arduously represented by its title), but a great deal has been written and spoken that could have been avoided if more writers on the subject (and its ramifications) were content with being disciples of Herder.

A.G.